SERVING
PRODUCTIVE
TIME

Stories, Poems,
and Tips to
Inspire Positive Change
from Inmates,
Prison Staff,
and Volunteers

Tom Lagana and Laura Lagana

Health Communications, Inc.
Deerfield Beach, Florida

www.hcibooks.com

Other books by Tom Lagana and Laura Lagana:

Chicken Soup for the Prisoner's Soul
Chicken Soup for the Volunteer's Soul
Serving Time, Serving Others
Touched by Angels of Mercy
The Quick and Easy Guide to Project Management

To arrange a seminar for inmates by Tom Lagana and/or Laura Lagana, obtain matching grants, free books with a purchase, and quantity discounts, visit www.TomLagana.com, e-mail Tom@TomLagana.com, or call 302-475-4825.

Library of Congress Cataloging-in-Publication Data

Lagana, Tom, 1944-
    Serving productive time / Tom Lagana and Laura Lagana.
      p. cm.
    ISBN-13: 978-0-7573-0782-9 (trade paper)
    ISBN-10: 0-7573-0782-5 (trade paper)
    1. Prisoners—Conduct of life.   2. Prisoners—Education.   3. Moral
education.   4. Spiritual life.   I. Lagana, Laura.   II. Title.
HV8869.L34 2009
365'.646—dc22

                                    2009002916

© 2009 Tom Lagana and Laura Lagana

All rights reserved. Printed in the United States of America. No part of this publication may be reproduced, stored in a retrieval system, or transmitted in any form or by any means, electronic, mechanical, photocopying, recording, or otherwise, without the written permission of the publisher.

HCI, its logos, and marks are trademarks of Health Communications, Inc.

Publisher: Health Communications, Inc.
                3201 S.W. 15th Street
                Deerfield Beach, FL 33442-8190

Cover design by Andrea Perrine Brower
Inside book design and formatting by Dawn Von Strolley Grove

What People Are Saying About
Serving Productive Time

"*Serving Productive Time* is a perfect intervention that we can depend on for participants and jail staff, because it engages people immediately and anyone can benefit from reading these stories."

—Morgan Moss and Penny Patton, codirectors and licensed therapists, Center for Therapeutic Justice

"I have experienced both sides of the razor wire. *Serving Productive Time* gives insight into the cast-off society of captives and sheds light upon the darkness called prison."

—Daniel S. Murphy, Ph.D., professor of political science and criminal justice, Appalachian State University

"Once, as a prosecutor, I was explaining to a young man that I was not willing to allow him to plead to any charge that did not require a mandatory sentence because I couldn't trust him to be good. His plaintive cry, 'I don't know how to be good' has never left me. The enormity of the issues that bring defendants to the justice system was evident in that statement. *Serving Productive Time* exemplifies how we can all work together to become better."

—Jane Brady, superior court judge

"*Serving Productive Time* gives us a rare glimpse into the minds and hearts of the incarcerated and waves the banner of hope and begs us to never give up!"

—Tammy Vega, administrator of volunteer services, Texas Youth Commission

"At a time in my life when I have no one, this book took my mind and heart to places I never knew existed."

—Jonathan Colabianchi, inmate

"From my experience, what people behind bars need is a belief in a higher power, family, friends, visits, programs, and inspiring books such as *Serving Productive Time*."

—Joan K. Johnson, mother of a former inmate

"Being incarcerated has beaten me down, but *Serving Productive Time* has shown me hope in action."

—Kenneth L. Hodge, inmate

"*Serving Productive Time* demonstrates that no matter what misfortunes have happened in people's lives, it is never too late to change and start anew."

—David E. Ritzenthaler, managing editor,
Prison Living Magazine

"This book illustrates the capability within all of us to embrace that which makes us human."

—Lori Brown, librarian

"With each story I thought, *just one more,* all the way to the end of this book."

—Joni L. Johnson, inmate

"*Serving Productive Time* presents the human side of those people who are doing time; both the ones who can't go home at night and those who can."

—David Winett, M.P.A., criminal justice
consultant and former warden

"*Serving Productive Time* reflects the real-life miracle of change when new awareness of self captures the spirit and mind. The reader will learn, grow, and feel hopeful that there are miracles at work, offering hope for tomorrow."

—Sylvia Sims Gray, Ph.D., professor,
School of Social Work, Eastern Michigan University

"*Serving Productive Time* is an outstanding collection of stories and poems from truly remarkable people."

—Aba Gayle, mother of murdered daughter

". . . inspiring stories and thought-provoking insight by a cross-section of people touched by incarceration, enriching our world on both sides of the razor wire."

—Jack Canfield, cocreator of the
Chicken Soup for the Soul® Series

With gratitude, love, and respect,
we dedicate this book to God,
inmates, former inmates, relatives and friends
of those imprisoned, prison personnel, volunteers,
victims of crime and their loved ones, and all
who make a positive difference behind the razor wire.

In memory of our contributing authors,
from this book and our previous books,
whom we grew to know and respect
and whose stories continue to leave
lasting impressions:

William J. Buchanan
Steven Dodrill
Bob Kennington
Ken "Duke" Monse'Broten
Rex Moore, Jr.
Derrick K. Osorio
Lou Torok

THE IN SIDE by Matt Matteo

Reprinted by permission of Matt Matteo.

It's important to find positive things to do in prison, whether it's reading, writing, drawing, weight lifting, running, or learning a foreign language. Exercise your mind, body, and spirit, and work on the core issues that brought you to prison in the first place.

Christian Snyder

Contents

Chapter 8: Discovering a Meaningful Purpose

Programs and Resources

Foreword

MARY V. LEFTRIDGE BYRD, deputy secretary,
Washington State Department of Corrections

Though I have been inspired to continue to serve in a profession, where the work is sometimes maligned and often misunderstood, I have never once been dissuaded from my calling. Embracing this profession requires boundless energy—physical, mental, and spiritual—in order to work toward a meaningful and sustainable impact.

I have had the opportunity to lead three prisons and two community corrections systems. It was during my second wardenship that I decided to manage the prison as a community, albeit a closed community. I determined we would base the daily operation on a community model, working and living as if we were somehow brought together to coexist in a relatively small community of 1,500 individuals. There were community standards that addressed a safe, clean, and orderly operation built on mutual respect, high levels of positive interaction, and I said it then and say it today, I did my best work for the institution by knowing and spending time with the external community.

No matter what one's station in life is, most of us have encountered enormous challenges and have been wounded in some way. Some of us bear wounds that weren't there at birth. More than a few of these wounds may have been caused by mean-spirited acts—disappointments that may have pushed us to the brink, causing grief for those who love us as well as ourselves. But these wounds may be a way of letting go and liberating our mind, body, and soul from the remnants of experiences we've carried around for too long.

All of us have spent some amount of time in the miserable camp called "You Reap What You Sow"! There is no disappointment like that which comes from self-generated wrongdoing. So what gets us back on track? How about finding the courage to stand up, stand alone, and admit the misdeed or poor decision? If you find the courage, many people may not stand with you, but if just one someone stands with you, you may well be on the way to moving forward.

Freedom, sobriety, and responsibility require constant attention. These are not events but processes—behaviors to learn and practice. If you are blessed to have support systems, you have possibilities. No longer will you be able to stand with one foot on Main Street and the other on Pain Street.

As you move forward—employed, involved in positive relationships, and rebuilding—never lose sight of those who cannot forget the impact you've had on their lives and how their lives have been changed forever by your path crossing theirs. The end of your service of sentence does not mark the end of the experience for crime victims and survivors.

No matter how well intended a person may be, old habits are never far away. You know, that little voice that whispers, "Come on, brother, have a little of this, take a little of that. Come on, sister, do this just one time." You have to dig your heels in and say, "No!" Say it loudly, like you mean it, acting deliberately for others to see you differently—to include that nagging little voice. You have to proclaim, "I'm running this. This is my life! I'm the holder of my fate! I am the restored owner of my life and soul, guiding my own choices!"

Perhaps you may have reached a time in your life when you finally "get it." In the midst of always living on the edge of crisis, along with fear and insanity, you stop dead in your tracks, and somehow that little voice is saying something different. It now cries out, "Enough! No more hustling, stealing, lying. No more daytime nightmares of your own creation." Something hits you. Blinking back the tears, you begin to see the world through new eyes. You realize it is time to stop hoping, waiting for something or someone else to change. You come to

terms with the fact that you are not all that you portray yourself to be. You are not perfect, and not everyone will love you
the way you want them to. Not everyone will appreciate,
accept, or approve of who you are—but that's okay, because
you have learned the importance of being your own champion.
At that moment, a sense of confidence will begin to emerge—
all you need to do is nurture it.

At this point you are ready to stop blaming other people for
the things they did to you or didn't do for you. You realize
people don't always say what they mean or mean what they
say, and not everyone will, or can, be there for you. You can
stand on your own and take care of yourself, and the result of
that process is a sense of security, which is the foundation for
self-reliance. You stop pretending, perpetrating, and judging
others. You begin to accept people as they are, and upon this
foundation, you add a sense of peace—born of forgiveness.
Next, you begin the process of sifting through and throwing
aside the junk you've fed to others.

Recognizing the need to open up to new thoughts and different points of view, you begin reassessing and redefining
who you are and what you stand for. You understand the difference between wanting and needing, and you begin to dis-
card the doctrines you've outgrown, realizing they never fit
you anyway. You begin to know there is power and glory in
creating and contributing. You realize the importance of setting boundaries and saying "No" like you mean it. The time
has arrived when something else can emerge from your life.

There are some who have not survived. They have paid the
price for their bad choices. Maybe this is your wake-up call.
At last, you stop agonizing over how you measure up. You
awaken to the tree of self-respect and the ability to accomplish—a tree that has branches laden with health, sobriety,
truth, balance, possibility, and yes, even love.

In order to achieve and sustain success, you need faith,

confidence, direction, and discipline. You cannot do this alone. Ask for help. You are prepared to step into and through your fears because you can handle it. To give in to fear is to give away the right to live life on your terms. You learn to fight for your life and not squander it by always having to look over your shoulder. Finally, you are ready to take a deep breath and begin to design the life you want to live.

We must talk until there are no more words, explain until all is understood, be honest until there is nothing left to hide, listen until everything is said, and question until we truly understand. Listen carefully as the voice of possibility rises above the noise of "us and them." You have everything it takes to live the life you have always imagined—a life that does not have to include police officers, prosecutors, judges, correctional officers, wardens, probation officers, or parole agents.

Let me return to where I started, as a public servant who has been a parole agent and warden—a public servant who has always been grateful for professional relationships with police officers, officers of the court, and social service professionals. Over the years, I have staked out a place for you at the corner of Hope and Healing. I invite you and others to join me there.

Any achievement or success I have known has been, without exception, a result of faith, meaningful relationships with family, friends, and staff, respect for self and others . . . and a belief that where there is life, there is hope. My hope extends to those who have survived crime; children affected by the absence of their incarcerated parents; thousands of criminal justice professionals who are experienced, practicing visionaries; faith communities and volunteers whose very presence helps public servants to deliver and enhance their ability to deal in dignity; and finally, my hope extends to those men and women who have learned, and will learn, to not simply serve time but to serve time productively.

Acknowledgments

Serving Productive Time has been a fast-paced, compelling, and gratifying project. We are grateful for everyone who assisted us, especially:

Our two treasured sons and their families who have blessed us with abiding love and continued support.

Mama Lagana, a one-of-a-kind role model who provided incredible insight and enduring encouragement for us to continue living our passion. May she rest in peace.

Douglas Burgess, Debbie Ellison, Brian M. Fisher, James Guy, Jacqueline Lagana, Ethel F. LeFave, Matt Matteo, Stella Shepard, Betty Strunk, Karl B. Strunk, Jan Singleton, and Corporal Carla Wilson, who not only reviewed and helped select the best material for our book but also provided valuable feedback relating to edits. They also connected us with additional authors whose work they felt should be included.

Jean Hull Herman, distinguished friend, accomplished poet, and published author, who shared her expertise by editing and offering suggestions on the poems.

We are grateful for each person who took the time to submit stories, poems, cartoons, and other fruits of their labor for consideration. While many were outstanding, not all of them were a compatible fit for the overall focus of this book.

We appreciate all who helped to make this book possible, in particular our contributing authors and cartoonists.

Everyone at Health Communications, Inc., for their continuing support in the publication and distribution of our books to prisoners throughout the world. In particular, Allison Janse and Peter Vegso, who believed in our project from the start; our managing editor, Carol Rosenberg; and Doreen Hess, for her patience, kindness, and help in distributing tens of thousands of our books.

The Inmate's Affirmation

JERRY GILLIES

These prison walls cannot contain my heart, mind, or spirit.

I deeply regret and forgive myself for any and all wrongs committed, and whatever damage I've done to all fellow human beings.

I forgive everyone who has misunderstood, persecuted, or abandoned me.

I am working toward the highest good for myself and others.

I am determined to leave prison a better person than when I entered—with hope, determination, compassion, and integrity.

I will fill each day of my incarceration with love, joy, and creative growth.

I will not allow my faith, inner strength, gentle spirit, or loving generosity to be damaged by this or any other hostile environment.

I am not a prisoner, but a temporarily contained, worthwhile human being waiting for my release, with lots to offer the world.

Introduction

Our purpose for bringing this book to fruition is not to honor prisoners or their crimes. Surely there is nothing honorable about life behind the razor wire. Nevertheless, there are hardworking people who, despite their circumstances, are making progress in carving out successful, new lives for themselves and others—from the inside out. Even though not all inmates will be released, some choose to serve out their time by making a world of difference from the inside.

We have four major objectives for publishing *Serving Productive Time*:

First, we hope that by reading this book, people will better understand that all of us are affected by incarceration. When people "mess up," countless others suffer the consequences—not only those who are locked up but also their families, members of their communities, coworkers, and others. From the prison across town to the clerk at the hardware store, from the halfway house down the road to the mechanic who repairs our cars, we unknowingly interact with people who have "done time." A neighbor's son or your best friend's wife might be serving time. Maybe Uncle Joe is a correctional officer. Every Sunday afternoon, Pastor Pruitt holds prison services at the county jail. Perhaps Ed, the jovial baker who made your birthday cake, served his debt to society years ago. The choices people make do have an impact on us all.

Our second objective is to inspire inmates to serve their "time" productively by making use of available programs and resources, performing positive deeds, and acquiring skills they can use on the inside during their incarceration, as well as after their release. We want to provide moral support to those who have a genuine desire to improve themselves while serving their "time" by spending quality time feeding their minds, bodies, hearts, and souls—namely, using their time to make constructive changes, such as learning new skills, coping with addiction, and seeking spiritual guidance, instead of simply wasting time. We hope this book will help raise the level of consciousness and encourage the implementation of additional programs and resources. In institutions where rehabilitative programs are scarce or nonexistent, we pray that the words between these pages will serve as a catalyst for establishing and enhancing effective programming, which will better prepare prisoners for a successful life on the outside, thereby helping to reduce the rate of recidivism.

Third, we want to empower correctional staff, counselors, volunteers, and others in a position to help the inmates who have a sincere desire to make positive changes in their lives, and/or to make amends for their transgressions. We also wish to provide hope to the families and loved ones of those incarcerated. No one should have to "go it alone."

Last but not least, we hope that all who read this book will gain a new perspective on those who are incarcerated and begin to understand their need for adequate preparation before returning to society as competent, contributing members of our communities. Some of our readers may even be inspired to facilitate positive changes within their own communities . . . to ultimately improve our imperfect world.

If there were such a thing as a "Wish List," the number one item would be for every correctional facility to release inmates who are better prepared to become productive citizens and contributing members of our society and to reduce the number of people who return to prison; or, better yet, to keep them from ever going there in the first place—especially our youth.

By inspiring others to serve their time productively to change for the better, and by making positive changes ourselves, together we can make the impossible possible.

Positive Influences

TOM LAGANA AND LAURA LAGANA

As we visit correctional facilities to present seminars to inmates, from time to time we have the added privilege of also addressing the charitable volunteers who willingly share their time and talents with the prisoners.

When we ask the inmates what impact these volunteers have on their lives, we find the perceptive answers are varied and always positive. Here are the top ten responses:

Volunteers:

1. Have a ripple effect on our lives.
2. Come with no ulterior motives.
3. Willingly share their experiences.
4. Give selflessly and expect nothing in return.
5. Help us look at ourselves differently.
6. Give us a feeling of self-worth by their mere presence.
7. Let us know that someone on the outside cares.
8. Share their wisdom—and it works both ways (reciprocally).
9. Create hope for new possibilities in our lives.
10. Bring us a new way of looking at life and especially ourselves.

By being courageous enough to tread behind the razor wire, volunteers represent a piece of the outside world, bringing with them not only positive energy but also possibly carrying the keys that will unlock the doors of understanding, atonement, growth, and change. Volunteers definitely have a positive influence on the lives of the incarcerated.

THE IN SIDE by Matt Matteo

Reprinted by permission of Matt Matteo.

❧ ❧

I think that through volunteer work and my job working in the law library, I was able to have a modest, but positive impact on the lives of others while I was incarcerated. It was a rewarding experience. We can remake ourselves and claim a new life.

Matt Bader

ONE

Sowing Seeds
of Wisdom

Should you find yourself facing a sentencing judge, as I was, and on your way to prison, resolve to come out of your ordeal wiser and better equipped to become an asset to your family, your community, and yourself. You can set goals and achieve them no matter who you are or how far you have fallen. Accept the fact that you are in prison and can't change that, and then find a way to prosper. Make your sentence a time to reflect, advance your knowledge, sharpen your skills, and increase your options.

GREGORY A. McWILLIAMS

First Impressions

GARY K. FARLOW

Like most people, I had a Hollywood image of prison: smoke-filled dormitories inhabited by tattooed body-builders carrying hate and homemade weapons. I arrived at North Carolina's Central Prison on a Friday evening. I wore my fear and trepidation like an aura as I, a pallid 128-pound weakling, stepped into my worst nightmare. It was like the old television commercial for E. F. Hutton. All conversation and card games came to an immediate halt when I walked into the dorm. All heads swiveled in my direction to size me up. My first thought was, *I'm going to die tonight*. I was about to learn just how misleading first impressions can be.

I never knew his real name. "Preacher" was probably in his late fifties and, despite imprisonment, carried the demeanor of one who hadn't a worry in the world. As fate would have it, I was assigned to the bunk immediately over him. After a couple of days of observing me in my self-imposed isolation, Preacher approached me carrying a soda and a Bible.

Now I always considered myself to be a Christian. I mean, I was brought up in the church, baptized, and "saved," so I must be a Christian, right? Yet, like so many, I tended to view God as some sort of "celestial Santa Claus" I called on only when I wanted something.

"You look like you could use a friend," were Preacher's first words as he handed me a Bible and a soda. My suspicions must have been obvious. Preacher tilted his head back and laughed. "Don't worry yourself. I ain't gonna hurt you, and I want nothing from you. My friendship and the Bible are free. You can repay the soda when you're able to."

My relief, as well as all of the anxiety and apprehension I'd kept bottled up inside, suddenly burst forth. Tears flowed, and my body slumped like a deflated balloon.

"You can live in prison one of two ways," Preacher explained. "You can serve time, or it can serve you."

Somewhat puzzled, I asked, "What do you mean?"

"Well, it's obvious. God intends for you to learn something. You have a choice now, just like you did when you committed your crime. It's called *free will.* You can spend your years consumed in anger, bitterness, and blaming everyone and everything else, or you can accept responsibility for your actions and make this time work *for* you and count for something."

"You mean, sort of like when life gives you lemons and you make lemonade?"

"Kinda," Preacher responded. "You have the opportunity, albeit forced upon you, to better yourself—get a handle on your problems, pursue an education, and develop a talent. It's all up to you."

I stared dumbfounded. I thought, *Is this guy trying to tell me to be grateful for prison?* "It sounds as if you think I should be thankful to be here, Preacher."

Shaking his head, Preacher replied, "No, Gary, not at all. What I'm trying to tell you is that you should make the conscious choice to not waste this time. Have something to show for it when the time comes."

Preacher left Central Prison just a few days later. As is the case, inmates are a transient population. When I think of him, I'm reminded of seventh-grade literature class and a book entitled *Brief Encounters*. It focused on the fact that we often meet people in our lives who we may know only for a short time but who have a lasting and profound impact on us.

Preacher was this sort of person.

That was nearly eighteen years ago. Since then I've earned a college degree, more than three hundred credit hours, and am currently pursuing a master's degree on an academic scholarship. I've published three books, a play, and innumerable short stories and poems. Equally, I've developed an appreciation for art that once upon a time I would never have taken the time for—all of this while making time serve me.

Most important, I've gained a greater sense of who I am and a deeper, more meaningful relationship with God. I no longer see Him as a celestial Santa Claus who I run to with a wish list of prayers. I now see Him as my Creator with whom I spend time every day.

Being in prison isn't easy. It still means being separated from those I love and hold dear. While I am still not grateful for prison, I have come to accept it and make serving time serve me.

❦

Each day brings me closer to the day I'll be out in the real world. In the meantime, I'm making the most of each day and using this time to my advantage in every way possible. It's only wasted time if I let it be.

Dave LeFave

Imagine

DAVE LEFAVE

Can you imagine a world without oceans or trees,
Where the wind doesn't blow, there's never a breeze?

Can you imagine a jungle made of concrete and steel,
Where you question your sanity and all that you feel?

Can you imagine changing your concept of what you call
    time,
Viewing it as punishment for committing a crime?

Can you imagine being searched, any time, any day?
You've lost all your liberty; you just do what they say!

Can you imagine a world fueled by hatred and rage;
You spend all your time sitting locked in a cage?

Can you imagine how it feels to be completely alone?
Enter this world, and you will surely be shown.

Can you imagine a world without kids and their play?
You've regressed to this place, and they force you to stay.

Can you imagine the eyes of a stranger, staring blankly back,
From a tarnished old mirror with an intrusive little crack?

Can you imagine being inspired in a world such as this,
Running the gamut to get back what you miss?

Can you imagine the haunting echoes of your yesteryears,
Or the strength you will need to face all your fears?

Can you imagine clinging to the dream that you're sure will
   come true,
Ignoring their criticizing all that you do?

Can you imagine the pride that you'd feel from within,
When you're expected to lose, and you suddenly win?

Can you imagine my world and the places I've been:
The who, the what, the where, and the when?

Can you imagine, for a moment, how it feels to be me,
Just sitting and dreaming about the day I'll be free?

*Return to your childhood and recall painful incidents
never forgiven. To be free of these negative burdens, it
is necessary that you forgive the offender. If confronting
the person might be harmful for either of you, visualize
yourself forgiving the offender. You might say to yourself: "[name of person], I forgive you. I pray that you
may be healed of the need to hurt others." You might
even thank the offender for a situation through which
you learned coping skills or to recognize behaviors you
would not want to inflict upon others. Without an
actual encounter, if you are sincere in forgiving, you
have been freed of the debilitating burden.*

Lois McGinnis
author of *The Way to Your True Self*

Inside My World

COURTNEY CHRISTINE SCHULHOFF

I am sixteen years old. I live in a place that has six bedrooms, each with its own bathroom, my own security, two conference rooms, and my own classroom. Some may say I've got it made. I must wake up to such luxuries every day.

You might ask, "What lottery did you win?" My answer, "I didn't!"

The life I wake up to every morning is the life of a juvenile inmate. My bedroom: one of six lockdown cells with one rusting, stainless steel toilet and sink. My security: one correctional officer and two surveillance cameras that observe my every move, twenty-four hours a day. My conference rooms: two private, tiny rooms where my attorney and I discuss the outcome of my life and one classroom where I study for my GED four and a half hours a day, Monday through Friday.

I am here because I made a horrible decision, and now I'm facing a life sentence. Some may say that decision was the biggest mistake of my life. I used to agree with them until an incredibly inspiring man, a volunteer who conducts a program here, told me that a mistake is not a mistake if you learn from it and move forward.

Every morning I wake up to the same disgusting food and feelings of loneliness. Every day is a struggle. I feel as though I'm using all of my energy to force myself to stay positive. I'm surrounded by people who treat me according to their "mood of the day" and who presume I am a lost cause. My tears flow freely. This is the harsh reality of incarceration.

Had I known months ago that my life would end up this way, I would have done everything within my power to avoid this awful world. I would have taken full advantage of my education and set goals that would benefit me in the long run. I would have surrounded myself with positive and aspiring people.

But I can't dwell on my "should haves," "would haves," and "could haves." I truly believe this experience is making me stronger and guiding me to where I must go and who I want to become.

To those who are reading this, you may be my age or have family members my age. I want to take this time to express and stress, especially to my peers, that life is too precious and rewarding to spend it in jail. Violence and drugs are not the answers. To every action there is a reaction. Only you can determine the outcome of your decisions. A positive decision leads to positive outcomes, and a negative decision leads to negative outcomes. It is up to you whether you want to be "looked up to" or "looked down upon."

Education, positive influences, and goals are the keys to success. Who do you want to be? Where do you want to go? Think ahead. Think of your future.

✼✼

My mistakes don't define who I am. My character consists of so much more than that horrible and seemingly unforgivable moment of despair, distress, stupidity, habit, abuse, or whatever led to it.

Michele Millikan
founder of *Prison Living Magazine*

THE IN SIDE by Matt Matteo

Reprinted by permission of Matt Matteo and Tom Lagana.

TTT/WWW (Things Take Time/We Will Win): This is an acronym I developed while imprisoned. It's simply true. Things worthwhile take time. With hard work there typically is a winning outcome. This mantra got me through prison, and I apply it in my life to this day.

Daniel S. Murphy

One in Thirty-Three

BOB PAULEY

Do you know me? I'm the one person in thirty-three who crosses your path every day that has been incarcerated in America's network of prisons at one time or another. I'm not a bad person, so have no fear. I just made some bad decisions in my life, perhaps only one, perhaps even none. It's estimated that upward of 6 percent of those incarcerated in America are actually innocent.

I'm the man who bags your groceries, the waitress who brings you coffee, and the kid on the bike down the street. I've been to your house before: as a plumber, an electrician, even the installer of your security system. I'm often unemployed because folks are scared to hire me. The fact that I've served my time and paid my debt to society sometimes makes little or no difference to them.

So maybe that's me, doing the temporary labor at the construction job. And likely you've seen me holding one of those "Will Work for Food" signs on the interstate ramp. That's not my choice, I promise you. It's just the way things turn out sometimes, no matter how hard I try.

I've been successful before, so maybe that's me at the bank counting out your money. Most often I've been broke, so more than likely that's me sweeping the carpet or carrying out the trash around town. One thing is certain: I *am* a part of your life. I cannot go away.

Do you know me? You may not realize it, but . . . yes, you do!

From Roadblocks to Stepping-stones

LAURA LAGANA

"A re we there yet?" During lengthy journeys in the car, my sister and I tried to outdo each other to see who could ask this question the most. No doubt we tested our parents' patience to the breaking point more than a few times.

Two weeks out of every summer our family returned to our Michigan roots, bonding with family and catching up on the news. Our time was divided between two cities, a hundred miles apart. We stayed with my father's closest brother and his family for the first week before moving on to my maternal grandparents' home for week two.

Almost every year, when we came to the outskirts of my uncle's town, we encountered a roadblock. Escapees from the nearby prison were notorious for hitchhiking along the only main road leading into or out of town, making it necessary for the police to stop and thoroughly search each car.

This meant my father had to empty the trunk. My research-chemist father was meticulous about everything. The task of removing the luggage from our car turned him into something resembling a disgruntled bear.

My earliest memory of an encounter with a police roadblock was around age five. I was terrified when the officer peered into the window of my father's car door. The policeman barked, "Everyone out of the car! You'll have to empty your trunk, sir."

Taking my sister and me by the hand, Mother gently

pulled us to the side and out of the way. Over and over I asked, "Why, Mommy? What happened?"

Each time she replied calmly, "A prisoner escaped, and they're trying to catch him."

My mind raced, taking my imagination along with it. I pictured a man in black-and-white striped pajamas popping out of our trunk with a ball and chain fastened securely around his ankle. Perhaps the idea came from the cartoons I watched on television.

Once we were repacked and back on the road, I was eager for answers to this puzzling event. "Daddy, why do people go to prison?"

In his wise, fatherly tone, he replied, "Maybe they don't have parents to love them like you do, pumpkin."

"What happens when they catch him, Daddy?"

My father scratched his head and furrowed his thick eyebrows, a sign he was thinking deeply. After a brief silence he said, "I suppose they'll have to put him in 'time-out' for a while until he learns his lesson."

"But, Daddy, how long will it take?"

He shook his head and answered, "I don't know, honey. I honestly don't know."

This experience took place fifty-plus years ago, but it's still fresh in my mind. My father's honesty and respect for others were two of his major strengths. Although my parents have long since passed through the pearly gates, I'm grateful for their guidance, wisdom, and open-mindedness. My father handled my inquiries with simple honesty and tact, without being judgmental or interjecting bias and his personal opinions.

It's probably no small coincidence that years later, in my role as a nurse, I would be taking care of a prison inmate in the hospital where I worked or that I would be visiting our local prison to attend a speech contest. I believe the roadblock of that long ago summer opened a tiny window in my heart and mind, planting the seeds of future possibilities.

Today I'm privileged to go behind the razor wire, together with my husband, as we conduct seminars, interacting and communicating with the men and women there, helping them to get their stories out to the free world and inspiring them to make positive changes in their lives. We encourage them to use their "time-outs" constructively to improve their minds, bodies, and spirits.

I realize that the challenges of corrections and attitudes about prisons and prisoners are far more complex than my father's simplistic "time-out" explanation. There are no straightforward solutions. But we can help prisoners remove the roadblocks to change and lay down stepping-stones to a productive and successful life. Together we will find an answer to the question: "How long will it take?"

Since my release, the greatest challenge I face is overcoming my criminal history. Some employers will not hire people who have a record, but others will. I continue to seek positive avenues for dealing with my past. Today, I continue to do on the outside as I did in prison: attend church, sing in the choir, and go to work every day. I hope to set an example for others on "how to do your time" and not let "time do you." To anyone who is incarcerated, I would say take all of the programs you can at your institution, seek an understanding of God, make amends to family and friends you have hurt, and prepare yourself to reenter society on a positive level with education and job training.

Reggie Holmes

Reprinted by permission of Charles Carkhuff.

Being incarcerated has given me the chance to learn about myself and ask questions like, "Where am I going?" and "What do I want to do with my life?" I have found out that the questions I ask myself are the ones that will save my life.

Clinton Avalos

Tough Questions, Honest Answers

SUELLEN FRIED

There are men and women in every prison who choose to "use" their time rather than simply "do" their time. Twenty-five years ago, I cofounded a self-help program for inmates in Kansas, "Reaching Out From Within."

Back then, our group decided to introduce ourselves to the community by offering an essay contest called, "The Ten Most Effective Ways to Stop Violence." We needed judges with experience and perspective, so we invited a group of inmates in a Kansas prison to select the best essay. A team of seven inmates read every essay and reached a unanimous decision. Enjoying the assignment so much, they asked for another. As a result of sponsoring a run around the baseball yard, the team managed to raise several hundred dollars for our program.

Now it was our turn for an assignment. The inmates requested the assistance of experts who could help them understand the source of violence in their lives. We brought in professionals to address the areas of child abuse, spouse abuse, anger management, conflict resolution, and other relevant topics. This formed the groundwork of our curriculum, which has blossomed into a self-help program run by inmates for inmates, and it's now in all eleven Kansas correctional facilities.

Since their inception, these discussion groups have brought about thousands of personal transformations. The program, sponsored by volunteers and supported by the Kansas Department of Corrections, meets weekly. Once inmates earn approval by their attendance in the program and demonstrate they are responsible for their own actions, they gain the privilege of speaking to high school students and juvenile offenders as members of the Inmate Speakers Panel. Their credo is: "You must be completely honest or you cannot speak to students again."

After arriving at the school or detention center, the inmates speak briefly about their crimes and their commitment to nonviolence before responding to a barrage of probing questions. The students' questions are often curious and sometimes cruel, but the answers are unfailingly honest.

The inmates are willing to deal with any subject they desire to dissuade even one student from making a choice that might result in imprisonment. They address the loss of privacy, the lack of choices about food, clothing, phone calls, and the shame they have inflicted on their families. The "hot seat" experience is invariably therapeutic for the inmates and their young audience.

I will never forget one exchange I witnessed at a suburban high school. The four inmate panel members began disclosing their convictions: drug dealing, robbery, sexual assault, and felony murder. The students wanted to know what the inmates missed most about losing their freedom and if it was possible to get drugs in prison.

One student asked, "Do you think your sentence is fair?"

His response, "Considering the number of crimes I committed before I got caught, I have no right to complain."

Even when the questions were cruel, the inmate panel answered each question with patience, respect, and honesty.

One conversation went like this:

"Who did you kill?"

"My wife."

"How did you kill her?

"With a gun."

"Do you have any children?"

"Two."

"Did you think about them when you shot their mother?"

"Not at that moment, but I have thought about them every day since, and I will for the rest of my life."

"How long have you been in prison?"

"Twenty-one years."

"Why did you kill her?"

"If I gave you an answer, it would be a justification, and there is no justification for what I did."

Little by little, the tone of the questions changed from confrontation to appreciation for the inmates' willingness to expose their innermost thoughts and deeds to a group of strangers. By the end of the hour, the audience seemed moved by the inmates' sincerity, whose only purpose was to make a difference in the lives of the students.

At the conclusion of the class, the inmate panel stayed to visit with anyone who wanted to continue the discussion. Tears flowed from both factions as the young students confessed and revealed serious problems in their own lives.

Inmates who participate in this program have a 11 percent rate of recidivism, compared to state and federal recidivism rates that can climb to 60 percent. If you sat in the back of the room when the panel appeared and witnessed the process that occurs for tough kids who begin the session with disdain for the losers, or righteous students with disgust for the guilty, you would observe human transformation in action—difficult to describe but amazing to experience.

Year after year, incarcerated men and women in Kansas lay their vulnerabilities on the line in hopes they will touch one soul and keep one youth from hearing the sound of the unyielding Iron Gate as it slams shut on the outside world.

Tasting True Freedom

TROY EVANS

The night of my release, my sister picked me up. For the first time in seven years, I was free. It felt strange to come and go at will. There were trees around me. I heard a kid laugh, and I had an ice-cream cone. To celebrate, my sister took me downtown for dinner and introduced me to sushi. The thought seemed repugnant, but compared to what I had been fed for years, I knew it couldn't kill me.

She dropped me off in town and went to park the car. There I stood: lights flashing, cars passing, crowds of people. The stimulation was overwhelming. It seemed like I was frozen in time. My sister approached and said, "You have a strange look on your face. You look fascinated and terrified."

The comings and goings of the free world were something I hadn't witnessed for years. I knew guys who returned to prison after purposely violating their parole because they couldn't take the real world. Having been told what to do and when to do it for so long, they couldn't make decisions. I heard stories of trips to the grocery store that would leave a grown man feeling overwhelmed only to realize that he had been standing in the aisle for an hour without making a deci-sion. I wondered, *Is this going to happen to me?*

Due to the circumstances of my release, there was no room for me in a halfway house. Instead, my parents went through an intense evaluation process to allow me to return to their home. At first I kept to myself, continuing the life I knew. I'd run in the morning, lift weights in the afternoon, and run in the evening. I filled the hours in between sitting at my desk, writing my résumé, and monitoring the stock market. I wandered aimlessly from room to room, unnerving my parents. They didn't know what to do about my empty stare—that made three of us.

Upon my release, I was aware that I would be on probation and be subjected to surprise inspections and ongoing scrutiny by a parole officer. Compared to another five years in prison, that seemed like a blessing. The eyes that kept me off balance were much closer than that. I was in my parents' home. The last time I had been under their roof, I was high, lying, stealing, disrupting the family, and breaking promises. Once I was locked up, I became easier to trust—but in the real world, with its temptations, no matter how hard they tried, they couldn't trust me.

I decided to embrace change and made a list of things I wanted to accomplish. I was committed. I spent every waking moment working toward something on my list, feeling compelled to prove to the outside world that I belonged. I thought I was being watched constantly, so it was paramount that I be seen as having focus.

One day I woke up and realized I had become the model prisoner all over again, despite my access to the outside world. I could walk barefoot through the grass, see a movie, and do anything I wanted, yet I hadn't allowed myself true freedom.

I started working at a local temp agency, began pursuing a future as a professional speaker, and found a mentor. Working in a furniture factory from 4:00 AM until 12:00 PM, doing their accounting, I'd head over to my mentor's place to put in another full day's work. Between the two jobs, I managed to save enough to buy a car—my first taste of freedom.

What I craved was my own space. I needed privacy, a place where I could go to sleep at night and feel safe, and a place where I could be alone with my new girlfriend.

From the moment I walked into my own apartment, everything clicked. I became more comfortable around strangers. I
could go to the mall and not panic. I started to change my persona from that of a con, on guard for the next life-threatening
event, to a free man.

For months, the things I craved most on the outside—
human interaction, normal conversation, and a safe environment—were outside of my grasp. I couldn't shake the
thousand-mile stare. Looking back, I think I had post-
traumatic stress. I couldn't put everyday things in the right
perspective. Groups of people were gangs, even if they were
eighty-year-olds with walkers.

Once I moved into my own apartment, that final shift took
place. Now I *wanted* to be around people. My girlfriend used
to tease me that I couldn't cross the room without stopping to
converse with a perfect stranger. I had been without normal
interaction for so long.

I found myself wondering why I had never realized how
special the world was, how beautiful flowers were, how sooth-
ing it was to lie in the shade. I was thirty-five, yet it felt like I
had never done these things.

My mentor took me aside and told me I was ready to begin
my own speaking career. Barely a year since my release, suddenly I was hopping planes, meeting more people in one day
than I would have thought possible. Groups paid me to tell my
story. I laid out my past for the public to scrutinize. To my surprise, they thanked me for making a difference.

This was the purpose of my journey. I had turned my life
around and was becoming the man I wanted to be. It wasn't
easy. I had to embrace change, but this time I had my friends
and family there for support.

Freedom was meant to be scary. I had to relearn it as a
sober, law-abiding citizen. Becoming educated and surviving
prison were only the beginning.

Dear You

TOM LAGANA

One cold November morning, I stopped by the emergency room of our local hospital to see if they could use my volunteer services. My official volunteer day was Thursday, but since I was already downtown that Saturday, I thought I'd offer to help out.

As I entered the triage area, one of the nurses waved and called out to me. "Tom, I need to see you after I check on my patient. I'll be right back."

"Sure, Nicole," I answered. "I'll be here." I couldn't help but wonder, *What did I do now?*

Minutes later she reappeared and explained, "I'm glad you're here today. My nine-year-old daughter decided to do a project on her own. It has to do with the Seven Corporal Works of Mercy."

Out of the blue, I had a flashback of my Catholic school days. "Sure, I remember them well. The nuns made us memorize them in grade school." I rattled them off in my head: *Feed the hungry, give drink to the thirsty, clothe the naked, shelter the homeless, visit the sick, visit the imprisoned, bury the dead.*

"Then you know that one of the corporal works is to visit the imprisoned. A few months ago, I recall your mentioning that you also volunteer at the prison. I want to ask you for a favor. My daughter wants to make Christmas cards for prisoners, but she doesn't know how to go about getting them to the inmates. Can you help us?"

"Of course. I plan to visit the prison before Christmas anyway, and I'm sending letters to inmates in other states. Her cards will be a welcome gift for everyone who has to spend Christmas behind bars."

"Thanks, Tom. She'll be thrilled. I can't wait to tell her." Then Nicole disappeared into another room to tend to her next patient.

The following Thursday, when I reported for my usual ER shift, thirty-one handmade Christmas cards were waiting for me, just as Nicole had promised.

Early the next morning, I sipped my coffee and read the cards with my wife, Laura. Each one-of-a-kind, handcrafted card was created on construction paper of various colors of the rainbow. They moved us to tears.

Dear You,

God watches over you all the time. If you turn your back on Him, He'll still be there and still protect you.

J.M.

Dear You,

You know how when you meet somebody, but you can't trust them? Well, you don't have to know God to trust Him. He'll never turn you down.

J.M.

Dear You,

You don't have to impress God. I'm saying that because usually people think they have to. Life is about making mistakes and learning from them.

J.M.

Dear You,

God has a plan for everyone. Maybe this wasn't His

plan for you, but this is just the beginning. Everything will be okay.

J.M.

Dear You,

I have faith in everyone. Maybe you did some stuff wrong, but everyone deserves a second chance. Even though I don't know you, I believe in you. For Christmas, will you do something for me? Pray to God. Merry Christmas.

J.M.

Dear You,

Never call yourself a failure. Yes, maybe you messed up in the past, but we all mess up. Hey, God is always there. Merry Christmas.

J.M.

Dear You,

You probably think badness is all around you. Well, look beyond the badness and see God standing there saying, "I love you." If you try hard, maybe you can see the same thing. Don't worry. God never takes a break.

J.M.

One week after sending out some of the cards, the responses began rolling in from inmates. Have a look at a few examples:

The first thing I want to do is tell you that I thought the Christmas card from the little girl was absolutely priceless! It warmed my heart when I got this, and I'd have to say that it was the best Christmas card I've ever received. Please be sure to tell her that I said, "Thank you." I showed it to several of the guys around here, and then sent it home to my parents.

Dave LeFave (Colorado)

That card from the little girl made me feel good. What a wonderful heart she must have to be so kind. In these places you learn to put your emotions in a box, but her card got through that wall I've built. It felt great to get behind that wall for a bit and feel the warmth she put there. I couldn't have asked for a better Christmas gift.

Charles Carkhuff (California)

The card from the little girl was so touching. Enclosed is my handmade thank-you note for the little girl who took the time and effort to make it. Please convey my gratitude to her mom as well.

John Schmidt (Delaware)

A nine-year-old made thirty-one cards like the one you gave me and wanted them all sent to prisoners? Wow! Must be quite a little girl to be so altruistic so early in life. When I was nine years old, I was busy dreaming about Luke Skywalker, not asking prisoners to pray. Makes me wonder what she'll become.

Matt Matteo (Pennsylvania)

Matt Matteo also enclosed an original drawing depicting an inmate on his knees, praying fervently in his cell. When I saw it, I was filled with emotion. Then, after turning the illustration over, I saw this notation:

Dear You:

Thank you for believing in me and for believing in giving second chances. I really value the card you made for me.

Thank you,
M.M.

Reprinted by permission of Matt Matteo.

❧ ❧

Peace Prayer of St. Francis

Lord, make me an instrument of your peace.
Where there is hatred, let me sow love;
Where there is injury, pardon;
Where there is doubt, faith;
Where there is despair, hope;
Where there is darkness, light;
And where there is sadness, joy.

Grant that I may not so much seek
To be consoled as to console;
To be understood as to understand;
To be loved as to love.
For it is in giving that we receive;
It is in pardoning that we are pardoned;
And it is in dying that we are born to eternal life.

The Vigilant CO

GEORGE T. SCANLON

There's a vigilant CO on this shift
That looks over here at me.
He watches all my movements,
Like a cat perched in a tree.
He gives me direction,
What to do, and I see,
That he bellows out orders
To protect me from me.

There's another man I talk to,
Who lives in my head,
I keep him in my prison,
Because he wishes I were dead.
He put me inside here.
He's my worst enemy.
And the vigilant CO
Protects me from me.

So I sit in my jail cell,
And pay back my debt,
And they pay out their tender
To keep me in check.
And the vigilant CO
That looks over me,
He goes 'bout his business
And protects me from me.

THE IN SIDE by Matt Matteo

Reprinted by permission of Matt Matteo.

🌿🌿

*All we have in prison is our word. Integrity means keep-
ing it. Some good examples of integrity are admitting our
faults, telling the next person when we are wrong, being
honest and respectful to the correctional officers, and
tolerating rejection. Integrity is simply doing the right
thing when no one, or everyone, is looking.*

John Schmidt

My Perpetual Protector

WILLIAM G. L. FRANCIS, JR.

My path to redemption and reformation began the day I was shot and taken into police custody. In the brief moments preceding the robbery, my intuition warned me that this particular bank robbery should not take place, and I should persuade my coconspirators to abort everything.

For the past seventeen years that I've spent in prison, I learned that my intuition is really part of the Divine Creator in me, playing the role of my perpetual protector—always vigilant, always true.

Life experience has taught me that as long as I continue to exist in human form, God and devil, right and wrong, good and evil, and heaven and hell are accessible to me whenever I prepare to make a decision.

From now on, my main focus will be on family and community for all the right reasons, because I believe God is most active and accessible in the midst of the loving family community dynamic. I'm solely responsible for my predicament, and I don't blame anyone—family member, friend, or associate—for my actions. If it is true that for every physical object or act there is a spiritual component, then it makes sense that I'm as guilty of criminal offenses against persons and property as I am of living far below my true potential.

Reprinted by permission of Gary K. Farlow.

Forgiving myself was a dilemma I struggled with for many years while in isolation. Everything I saw reminded me that I made a serious mistake, and I saw nothing that allowed me to be forgiven of that mistake. Forgiveness came for me only after I left isolation and could walk freely around the compound and meditate on what I had done. When I was able to ask GOD to forgive me, then I was able to forgive myself.

Stella Shepard

Become a Sponge: Soak Up Life's Lessons
TOM LAGANA AND LAURA LAGANA

1.1 What are the following people trying to teach you? What have you learned from each of them?

   a. Mother:

   b. Father:

   c. Sister:

   d. Brother:

   e. Counselor:

   f. Prison Volunteers:

   g. Correctional Officers:

   h. Roommate:

   i. Fellow Inmates:

   j. Former Inmates:

   k. Spouse/Loved One:

   l. A Close Friend:

  m. Others:

1.2 How can you set a good example for others?

TWO

Family Matters

Being separated from my family in such draconian fashion has made me appreciate them all the more, to never take them for granted as I once did in my youth. Today I hang on their every word and deed, as though it may be the last time we speak. During more than two decades of incarceration, I've lost all but one of my grandparents. The number of regrets for things left unsaid are too numerous to count. Now I don't waste a moment I have with my family. To me, they are even more precious than my freedom.

DOUGLAS BURGESS

Dime-store Paper

JAY ANGELO

One letter from my son stands out most in my mind. It arrived three years ago. He was eleven years old, and I was three years into a four-and-a-half-year stretch in the hole.

When the second-shift officer slid a few letters beneath my door, I had no idea how my life was about to change. I scooped them up and rifled through them to see who had taken time out of their day to connect with me. One letter was from a friend serving time at another prison, the next was from my father, and at last a letter from my son.

The sight of my son's squiggly handwriting filled me with joy. I hastily read my other letters before I sat down to savor my son's letter. My heart sputtered like an old jalopy as I opened the envelope and read his bold words: "Mom told me why you're in jail. Please don't sin, Dad. Jesus watches what you do. Pray to Him."

I stared at that small paragraph for what felt like hours. My body trembled violently as everything inside of me threatened to break in half. It was the first time I'd given any thought to the fact that my son would grow up to see me as a prisoner and a sinner. His words forced me to examine things about my life that I'd wished would quietly vanish.

It was never my intention to hide my past from my son. Instead, I wanted to be able to sit down and explain it to him when I felt he was old enough to understand. Then reality slapped me in the face, and the pain of not knowing what to say spread through my body. I didn't know the context of the conversation between him and his mother. *Did she sit down and explain it to him as she tried to explain my absence? Did she tell him to make him feel bad?*

Because I didn't know the answer, I didn't know how to respond. The only thing I was sure of was the fact that I'd have to do all in my power to turn my life around. It was the only way I could show him that I wasn't a monster. I also thought about my victim's family. I'd robbed them of their father, husband, and son. If all I was supposed to be in life was a murderer, then both of our lives would be in vain. I didn't want that for either of us.

My life in prison was not a game and neither was the life I'd taken. I knew that I had to use my incarceration and my crime to reach out to at-risk youth to help them change their lives, especially my son's life.

As I continued to read his letter, I knew I had to get my life together and do all I could to be a better person, father, brother, and advocate of nonviolence in the inner city. My son's words shredded my thoughts like confetti and scattered them across the cold cell floor. With each sentence he scraped away the scar tissue of emotional indifference that had accumulated over the years. On dime-store paper, he carved a piece of hope and determination into my heart, touching me in places that only a child could reach. His candor made me smile. He wasn't hindered by pretense or arbitrarily imposed ideas of right or wrong. I loved his forthrightness. I thought, *I owe him the truth, but more than this, I owe him a father*.

His letter continued, "Daddy, I wonder how you're doing in there. I'm doing fine. When I think about you, it makes me feel sad. With no daddy around to help out and to be strong, I have to do things all by myself. I miss you. I pray one day my prayer will come true, and we'll be together for life. The anger in my heart hurts me the most. Mama says I'm the man of the house. She says I have to control my anger so I won't be in jail, too."

My son's words made me feel small in a place where I'd been made to feel important. His words knocked the facade of hood-toughness and prison savvy right off my face. No glory was to be found among the ruins that constituted my reputation. The crime I'd committed was no badge of honor in his eyes. It was merely a scarlet letter identifying how badly I'd failed him and all the young black males in my neighborhood who would die or spend their lives in prison for emulating me. Years before I'd acknowledged my guilt, but there was a difference between that and facing up to the consequences of my actions. My son's words forced me to accept responsibility for the life I'd taken.

When I finished reading his letter, I was terrified for my son and all the young men who had fathers like me—fathers who were languishing in prisons as their sons were growing up, fighting the anger that threatened to consume them. I thought reaching them would be a way for me to take responsibility.

I sat down and grabbed a pen. Dipping the tip of the pen into the tears that danced down my face, I began writing to my son, desperately explaining to him how and why I came to prison. I made a vow to him that I would never kill again. As I wrote that promise, I realized I could never rationalize taking a life. So I did my best to explain to him what it felt like to be a confused teenager under the influence of liquor and anger.

I was responsible for a senseless act of violence that shattered many lives. In my heart, I hoped my son and I could pick up the pieces and patch them back together. I wrote until I was emotionally and spiritually drained, yet I felt better than ever.

My son and I continue to correspond, and with each letter our relationship grows. When I wrote warning him of the dangers of drugs, cigarettes, and alcohol, he responded weeks later, when we spoke on the phone. "I'm an athlete, Dad, and so are the guys I hang with. Those things would keep me from reaching my goals." I smiled proudly as I listened, comforted by the knowledge that our letters were meaningful.

The messages we send to each other not only connect us but also challenge us to grow in ways I could never have imagined.

Reprinted by permission of Matt Matteo.

Mom and Dad

DAVE LEFAVE

I write these words for you, Mom and Dad,
To provide some comfort when I know you're sad.

There's nothing magical that I can say
To make what has happened go away.

I wish somehow I could explain
The reason for all of this needless pain.

But there are no answers when we ask ourselves why.
Just don't ever think it's because you failed to try.

Everyone knows that this simply isn't true,
And that you always did what good parents do.

You taught me morals and to be polite,
You came and held me in the middle of the night.

There was food on the table, a roof over my head,
Love and compassion whenever tears were shed.

You showed me the difference between right and wrong,
To never give up and always stay strong.

I only wish that I could change the past
By slowing it down, because it went too fast.

Now, Mom and Dad, I'm sitting here in this cell,
With the words of a poem trying to tell

About the love that I have for you deep in my heart,
And the pain that I feel because we must be apart.

I can only imagine how tough it must be
For both of you having to see

The road that I've traveled over the years,
So self-destructive and causing your tears.

I just want you to know that however this ends,
You are much more than parents, you're also my friends.

All my love,
David

*One significant thing that our son did during his incar-
ceration was to call his dad and say, "Dad, I need you."
His dad needed to hear that, and from then on, they
were able to rebuild their relationship. I don't think my
son would ever do anything again to lose his father's love.*

Ethel F. LeFave

Just Be a Parent

GRACE CLARK

Our youngest, a high school senior, was among the musicians chosen to provide entertainment for the inauguration of our new governor at the governor's mansion. As typical proud parents, we told everybody to watch the news so they could catch a glimpse of our daughter on TV.

On that same day in January 1979, our oldest was arrested. South Florida citizens had been locking their doors for a week, while TV journalists tracked the progress of the police investigation concerning the latest local crime. In spite of everything, we loved our son.

Reporters specifically assigned to this case at the *Miami Herald* and the *Palm Beach Post* printed extensive articles. Headlines in the metro section read, "Methodist Minister's Son Arrested." Our secret was out.

We didn't know a soul who had gone through anything like this before. *What's going to happen? What can we do?* This was a foreign world we knew nothing about. We kept to ourselves, and I locked the secret deep within my heart.

I only told my brother, who lived in Massachusetts. I chose to be isolated from accusations and criticism, but deep inside I longed for some friends. Nobody phoned. Nobody visited. Nobody cared.

Two days went by. Then on the third day, while I was home alone, our bishop called. He opened Pandora's box with a simple statement of genuine concern. "Tell me about your situation, Grace."

Through tears, I explained, "We're at our wit's end. How do we find the right lawyer? Do we take out a loan for our son who was arrested when we didn't take out loans to help our other children who needed tuition? We don't have much savings. We know nothing about jail and incarceration. Here we are, both trained to counsel, yet we don't have the slightest idea how to handle this. We just don't know what to do!"

We felt rejected. Our lives had been tainted. The bishop listened in silence. When I was finished, he offered this sage advice, "You just need to be his parents."

As we prayed, I was able to turn it all over to God and accept the role of parent. I believed that He knew who would be the lawyers and judge, and that they would be specially chosen. And they were. God made better selections than I would have.

Within a few hours of the bishop's phone call, several parishioners visited our home. They became our support. It was good to have people to talk to about our secret. Our son served a lengthy sentence in jail and then in the state prison system. Through it all, we finally stopped acting like a minister's family and became what he needed the most: his parents.

[EDITOR'S NOTE: *Kairos Outside is a support group for the families of men and women who are or have been incarcerated. For information, see www.kairosprisonministry.org or contact 130 University Park Drive, Suite 170, Winter Park, FL 32792.*]

❧❧

Tears fall during the silent darkened hours when our bodies can't move from our bunks. If we do, we are considered to be out of place and could go to the hole.

Stella Shepard

The Best a Mom Can Do

BELINDA PITTS HARRISON
as told to Tom Lagana and Laura Lagana

It has been eight years since my son went to prison. It seems like forever. No one understands how much my heavy heart hurts. I don't think God hears me anymore. I was alone the day my son went to prison. I walked into the house, fell on my knees, and cried until there were no more tears. I cried every day for the first three years.

After most visits, I sit in the hallway outside the prison visiting room and cry in front of the officers and visitors—but never in front of my son. I must be strong for him and for his son. Steven went to prison just as he became a father. His son, now eight years old, loves his dad. Both of them are missing out on so much.

During our visits my son isn't allowed to walk around, and we aren't supposed to touch, except when we enter and leave. We are permitted to purchase snacks from a vending machine and share them.

It was four years before my son was allowed to have his picture taken. My grandson learned his colors with M&Ms. At the prison he learned how to count. Even though Steven wasn't allowed to handle money, he pointed at each coin or bill as my grandson proudly announced the name and amount.

Our family has changed a lot since my son went to prison. My oldest son got hit by a car and was in the hospital fighting for his life. During this time, Steven was being processed to serve his sentence. My younger son got married and had two children. My daughter married and moved twelve hours away. After twenty-three years, I divorced. It was as if a bomb shattered our home, and we all ran in different directions.

I still weep because I can't help my son. There is no greater pain than to watch your offspring suffer. If only I had known that sometimes the best thing and the hardest thing we can do for our children is nothing.

Steven once said to me, "Thank you for coming to visit, for sending me money when you can, and for your letters, Mom. It means so much, especially your visits."

"I'm your mother," I said. "That's what mothers do, and that's why I'm here."

He responded, "No, Mama, that isn't why. You're extra special. Many mothers never come here. I thank God that you're mine."

I never thought my son would be taken away. He grew up in prison. With all my heart, I want my son to come home. Sometimes, in the middle of the night, I picture him in that cramped cell and wonder, *Why?*

There are so many things I want to share with others who may be going through similar circumstances. I want children to understand, not only their own pain, but the pain they cause their families.

My son has attention deficit disorder. He had trouble in high school and didn't finish. Now he helps teach GED classes at the prison. I only hope God will let Steven come home before prison is all he can remember.

The Shape of an Angel

JAN SINGLETON

Visitors at Oregon State Correctional Institution drive up to an intercom and announce why they are there. After being instructed to take a number, they are permitted to drive to the visitor's parking lot where they wait in their cars for their numbers to be called.

This prison is situated in the middle of a flight pathway for migratory birds. Almost always, you can see small clusters of birds soaring overhead. One Sunday afternoon, as I sat in my car waiting for my number to be called, I glanced over toward the institution. Something remarkable caught my eye.

I noticed a large group of birds take flight. As they neared the prison, they split from their original pattern, forming the shape of an angel. I felt cold chills from head to toe. You see, for me that was a personal affirmation that the Lord was indeed answering my continuing prayer: "Lord, please send your angels round about my son to create a hedge of protection."

After what I had read and heard about the things that can befall a person living in prison, I used to worry a great deal about my son's well-being. Since that Sunday, I look for the birds whenever I visit my son. I know he is in good hands.

Faith is to believe what you do not yet see; the reward
for this faith is to see what you believe.

St. Augustine

You'll Never Cry Again

RAY BENICH

My only child died suddenly on March 4, 1997. After a brief struggle, Bradley succumbed to cancer at the tender age of twenty-one. They allowed me to talk to him on the phone from the counselor's office here at the prison. That was the last time we spoke.

He sounded sedated. "Hi, son. Did you just come from chemotherapy?" I asked.

"Did Gram tell you I have cancer?" He begged his grandmother not to tell me that he had cancer because he didn't want me to worry. That's the kind of noble child he was. In spite of being callously informed by the doctors that he was dying and only had a short time to live, Bradley was adamantly opposed to anyone telling me of the seriousness of his condition.

I struggled, adrift on my own sea of grief, to deal with this under the imposed communal conditions of incarceration. Yet, on another level, just days after Bradley's death, I realized a sense of relief. As a creative outlet, I felt inspired to express my grief by writing these lyrics:

> *All those years that we were apart, I kept you close within my heart, prayed every night, that you'd be all right, and that God would bring you back to me.*
>
> *And now, you'll never cry again.*
>
> *That final letter you never sent, found only now mistakenly. It touched me deeply. It comforts me . . .*

*my only child . . . my loving son. You too are my
"best friend,"*
   And now . . . you'll never cry again.

   *You're in His care. Someday I'll be there. No one
will take away what we will share. When all time
has passed, I will be free . . .*
   And you'll never cry again.

   *Never again will we be apart, your broken heart
. . . a joy so brief. Day after day, I embrace the grief.
Somehow I carry on as best I can. Yet thoughts of
you crash over me, like waves of joy and misery.
Remembering as I always will, that one brief hour
that we shared that day . . . still kept apart and
locked away. Their cold hearts could not be touched
. . . but my son, you'll never cry again.*

   *Steel and glass couldn't separate, divide or con-
quer, nor penetrate our love, our dreams, the plans
we made. That one brief hour we shared that day,*
   And now, you'll never cry again.

❧ ❧

*I saw hope for my future reflected in my son's image of
me. Once I caught a glimmer of that hope, I began to
see it when I looked at the reflection in the mirror. He
taught me that. He taught me to start believing that anything was possible again. He taught me to live my life
with the hope of a child.*

Troy Evans

Sunlight of My Soul

LELAND J. BALBER

Now I'm not claiming that the experience I'm about to share with you is unique—in fact, I believe there are countless parents, brothers, sisters, family members, and friends facing this same nightmare.

At the end of January 2006, I came to this camp. I'm a fifty-eight-year-old man with two adult offspring, ages twenty and twenty-two, and a Labrador retriever. They have been the core of my life and the joy that makes my life worthwhile.

Three months after I came here, I was notified by my son and my brother that my daughter had died of a drug overdose. My heart was broken. Not only was I in a place that provided me with no time or opportunity to have been there for her, to once again try to save her from the grip of a terrible disease, but I was allowed no time or opportunity to mourn my loss.

To deal with my grief and provide a way for me to mourn and slowly let go, I write letters to my daughter almost every day. These letters express my sadness, anger, love, helplessness, and a host of sentiments that allow me to work through my grief. I hope and believe that the following letter can help others find peace in their grief—and perhaps stop others from plunging into the same abyss once they realize the impact their behavior will have on those who love them.

Here is one of my letters:

Saturday, October 28, 2006

Dear Liz:

Another Saturday night around the old campfire. Just kidding. It's really another night here in the prison library. I was just talking to a friend who's teaching me Spanish. We were discussing a word that has been rolling around in my head today. The word is *despedirse*, which means "to say good-bye."

I realize that in all of my letters to you, this is what I have not done yet. I didn't get to say good-bye before you left because I never, in my wildest imagination, thought that I wouldn't see you or talk to you again. Well, here I am, and I don't even know where to begin. I guess I should first tell you that I don't want to say good-bye. If I could, I would hold on forever.

You see, saying good-bye seems to have such finality. I can't imagine my world without you in it in some way. Maybe I'm holding on and not letting something, the next something, come to me. Maybe if I can say good-bye, I'll be more open to reaching a better spiritual connection with you. I won't have such a hard time dealing with my memories because I keep embracing the pain, and it blocks out all of the good feelings from the joy you brought into my life. I can't even write lyrics to a song without becoming overwhelmed with emotion. I have to stop.

Yet I'm not quite ready to say good-bye. I'm holding on for dear life; I'm afraid that I'll drown in a sea of sorrow if I open the floodgates by saying good-bye while I'm here. Maybe when I'm home, safe and surrounded by friends with your brother there, I'll be better equipped, probably just more willing and less able, to deal with my feelings.

But to say good-bye to you . . . it seems I just said hello. It was not that long ago when you came into my life, and I thought you would be here forever—not for me, but for sure you and your brother, Zack. Now I'm supposed to say good-bye? Unthinkable.

So, for tonight, I can only get around to saying, "See you later." With all my heart and soul, I hope to see you again, in a better place, without the pain you suffered. You give new meaning to the concept "sunlight of my soul," for that is what you truly are. Always know that I will love you with all of my heart and soul until the end of time and then some.

All My Love,
Dad

When I think of all the things I'd like to do when I'm free, the first thing that comes to mind is being able to just sit at home and talk with my mom again. That is one thing that I will admit prison has taught me—it's those things you never think about while you're free that are truly valuable.

Matt Matteo

What Do You Tell a Crying Mother?

KEN "DUKE" MONSE'BROTEN

Just got a letter from an old cellmate's mother. She writes the standard greetings, tells of her problems, getting to work during a cold spell we just had, and a few complaints about the prices of things these days. Finally, near the end of the letter, she tells me of going to see her son in Washington State Penitentiary a few days before. She tells me that he is okay, not "good okay," she stresses.

He seems different, and she wonders if there is a possibility of him trying to kill himself. Then she tells me that two members of her family have committed suicide in the past and that if her son did the same thing, it would kill her.

His mother had never written me before. She knew very little about me other than that I was in the same cell with her son for a few months in the past. She has only one son, had never been exposed to the prison system before, and now she was confused and scared for him. She was asking for an answer to something I could only guess at.

It was the same old story as far as her son went. He was angry at being reduced to a number, a security rating, and being treated as subhuman. He was acting differently because he was different. His mother saw these changes as depression, and she was right.

I could tell her that her son would be his old happy self again as soon as he settled down a bit within the system and got used to things, but I knew different. He would only get better at hiding his anger, masking his hate with a smile, and even laughter. As far as killing himself, that was anyone's guess. Most first timers don't, but it happens.

Since he had a family history of suicide, I'm sure the odds were not as good as they might have been. I knew too that if this mother told this same story to prison officials, by phone or letter, her son would be placed on suicide watch in the hole and a record of it would become a part of his permanent file.

So, what do I tell this crying mother? Do I tell her to pray? Darn right, she better do that. Do I deepen her fear by telling her the truth? Do I tell her that her son is now inside a beast that knows only numbers? No, I think not.

I can't tell her about my own experiences within the system. How do I tell a crying mother that her only son, the little boy her heart and soul needs, the boy who has never been away from her for more than a few weeks at a time since he was born, is being turned into a very angry man with a 77.7 percent chance of returning to prison? Instead, I write the following:

Dear Mrs. Shea,

Thank you for a great letter. Sorry to hear about the frozen streets and ice in your area; you better be careful. So you got to see Sonny at the walls. Kinda looks like an old castle or something, doesn't it?

I'm sorry to hear about your concerns in regards to Sonny. He is a good, strong kid, both mentally and physically; you should be very proud of that fact. He is going through some very different and changing times right now, so he could be depressed at times. We all go through it when we first get to prison.

I've just finished a letter to him. I told him to get into school, to attend any and all meetings where he can meet people from the outside who come in as guest volunteers. I told him to get into sports and to watch TV a lot, instead of letting his mind run wild in his cell. I told him to attend church as much as he could. I also explained to Sonny that the three biggest enemies he has right now are sheer boredom, social arrest, and the anger that comes from being constantly degraded.

I also told him to give his mother a break—that she is doing time just like he is and feels even more helpless than he does. So, in closing, let me just say that I understand your feelings, and the best advice I can offer is to write him often, even if it's only a card, send him ten dollars once in a while, and let him know that he is still loved very much. That will give him the strength he needs so badly right now.

Respectfully,
Duke

Guess that makes me as bad as this beast for not having the heart to tell the truth to this crying mother. As bad as I hate it, I find myself protecting others from truly knowing the vicious, uncontrolled monster prison has become, out of shame for what it really does to their loved ones. Hopefully, my own family will never know what I too have been forced to experience in prison. There are too many crying mothers out there already.

As a parent of an inmate, I still ask myself, Why did things happen this way? *The only answer I can come up with is: it's God's plan.*

Ethel F. LeFave

What Do You Say?

TOVA LANGLEY

What do you say to a four-year-old who says to you, "Mama, you're in jail"? That's what my son said to me one night on the phone after being in prison for thirty months. With three months left before I can go home, I try to laugh it off and convince myself that he's too young to really under stand what he's saying.

What do you say to your child when you have to see each other through bulletproof glass, and he wants to know why he can't come and sit on your lap? Do you tell him you were bad, and that's why you have to be here? So he's scared to death that if he's bad, the cops are going to come and get him too? Or do you look your innocent child in the eyes and lie?

What do you say when your child asks why he had to be quiet and hide when the cops were knocking on the door? Something that you wrote off long ago because you were sure he was way too young to remember that.

What do you say when, day after day, your child asks you, "Mom, when are you coming home?"

What do you say?

Why, Daddy?

ROBERT A. WOODRING

My wife and I picked up our seven-year-old son about noon. It was a warm, overcast day, and the chance for rain increased by the minute. Our son had been living with his aunt due to a ruling by the courts. I was still able to see him and call him anytime I wanted. He just had to live with his aunt for now. As my wife and I got him into the car and buckled his seat belt, I asked my son, "Is there any place special you want to go?"

He quickly answered, "Yes, Daddy, that golf and games spot we always go to as a family."

We arrived just as it began to rain. For hours we kept our son content with various games. I tried to conceal what I was about to tell him. Keeping it inside tore me apart. This wonderful little man was about to have his world come falling down.

As I peered out the car window, I noticed the rain had ended. I took his hand, and we walked outside. We looked up to see a tremendous rainbow stretching across the sky. I looked up to the heavens, knowing this was the right time, and said a silent prayer, *Thank You, Lord, for the strength I need.*

My son and I walked over to a rain-soaked bench. I took off my jacket and draped it across the soggy surface. He and his mother sat together as I stood before him. There he was, our beautiful blond-haired, blue-eyed little man, so full of love and life. As his mom took his hand, a lump formed in my throat and my eyes began to well up with tears.

"Son, I need to tell you something, and I need you to be a very big boy now," I began. He sat up straight, and his smile began to fade. "Daddy is going to have to go away for a while, and I won't get to see you, maybe for a long time." My words were like knives cutting away pieces of my heart. I could feel each one take its share. "I won't be here to play with you or do much of anything else with you for at least five years."

Tears slid down his cheeks—a vision I see each night of my life as I lay down to sleep. The tears fell, one after another, and then came the words I dreaded. "Why, Daddy?" he asked through his flood of tears.

My wife grabbed our son and held him tight. I fell to my knees. I was afraid to say anything, but I knew I had to compose myself. As I looked into his eyes, red from crying, my heart broke. The words stuck in my throat, but somehow I managed to choke out, "Because I broke the law, and when grown-ups do something wrong and break the law, they go to jail—sometimes for a long time."

He looked at me with incredible insight for a seven-year-old. There was nothing in the world that could have prepared me for that moment. We sat together on that bench for more than an hour, holding one another, telling each other that it would be okay and not to worry.

The time to return him to his aunt came so quickly, it seemed unfair. When the moment came for me to say good-bye, I looked up to God. I was afraid to let my son be drawn to tears again. When his aunt came to take him back, I made sure my son was securely buckled in her car and thanked her once again. As I prepared to walk away, I thought about his future. *What is he going to do without his father? How will he turn out? How will he handle not seeing me anytime he wants?*

Then all of those thoughts faded when I heard him say,

"Bye, Daddy, I love you. See you soon!" Even in this little man, there was something I never expected to hear—hope and faith.

Since my incarceration, many things have happened to me. I lost a brother and mother to violent deaths. My wife left me. My two oldest children have disowned me. I have been beaten more times than a poor prizefighter, but through it all, my son and I have continued to write each other. At the end of every letter remains my hope, as he concludes with, "See you soon, Daddy. I love you."

❦

THE IN SIDE by Matt Matteo

Reprinted by permission of Matt Matteo.

The Power of Music

ANN EDENFIELD SWEET

Tony called yesterday. He is eleven years old. His stepsister is in a correctional facility in Grants, New Mexico.

I met Tony and his parents one Saturday when we rode together in the church van to the Wings Valentine's Day party. While we rode, we played mixer games so we could get to know one another. Then I started teaching the songs we planned to sing at the party.

Tony paid such close attention that I had to ask him, "Want to help me lead the music once we arrive at the prison?"

"Wow! You mean it?" His reply was confirmation enough.

Tony sang along with me and helped demonstrate the gestures to the more than 350 inmates and guests in attendance. Tony and his parents come from a small town in northern New Mexico. Since their old car was unreliable, they rode the sixty-two miles to the prison with us. They caught a ride back to their car in Albuquerque with another woman from their hometown. She followed them for the remaining 100 miles to make sure they got home safely. It was regrettable for me, because I didn't have a chance to talk with Tony or his parents after the event.

Two days later Tony called. "Could you please mail me copies of the music for the songs we sang?" He explained that he had been given an old guitar. When he tried to teach himself how to play and sing the songs, he realized he needed the music.

"Sure, Tony. I'd be glad to. I haven't had a chance to talk with you about the party. What did you like best?"

"It was the music!"

As I spoke with his mom the next day, she remarked, "You should see Tony. He's been singing those songs since we left the prison, and that's not all. He's teaching his friends, too. They've learned all the words, and now they want more. I don't recall when I've seen him this happy. I don't know how to thank you, Ann."

"I'm happy he's so passionate about music," I replied. "I just hope and pray that I'm making a small difference in his life."

Tony's grandfather, father, two stepsisters, and one stepbrother have all been in prison; yet Tony went into a prison and came out singing songs that praise God. Now he's sharing them with his friends in rural New Mexico.

When I told this story to my friend, owner of a radio station, he told me he would like to put Tony and his friends on the air. I called Tony and told him the news, adding, "When you and your friends have rehearsed enough and are confident in singing on the radio, my friend at the station has invited your team to perform. How about that?"

"Thanks, Ann. We're already working on one special song."

Perhaps Tony's interest in music is powerful enough to help him avoid the family pattern of incarceration. Even though his story is still unfolding, his positive actions are already changing his young world.

[EDITOR'S NOTE: *For more information on Wings Ministry, write to 2270 D Wyoming Blvd. NE #130, Albuquerque, NM 87112-2620; e-mail: information@wingsministry.org; website: www.wingsministry.org; phone: 505-291-6412.*]

A Man of Integrity

ROY A. BORGES

Pop looked at his calendar. "June 17 falls on a Sunday," he said.

"Thanks, Pop," Joe replied.

Everyone called him Pop. His hair was almost entirely white. It didn't bother him anymore, though. At fifty-eight, he didn't feel like a pop. When he was on the handball court, no one thought he was a pop either. He played like he was twenty-something.

"Hey, you know what else the seventeenth of June is?" Pop asked.

"No," Joe responded from the top bunk.

"It's Father's Day. It falls on the third Sunday in June."

"Yeah, I knew that," Joe said.

"I bet you didn't know why and how it became a legal holiday."

"No, Pop, can't say that I do."

"Back in 1909, William Smart's daughter was listening to a Mother's Day message in her church. Louise Dodd wanted to honor her father, not for what he did, but for what he was."

"And what was he?" Joe asked.

"A man of integrity who practiced what he preached. He followed God with his actions—not just his words."

"I wish I had a dad like that," Joe replied. "I've never had a meaningful relationship with my father. I love him, but I've never felt the sense of belonging that comes when you know you're valued . . . not because of what you do or don't do, but because of who you are. You know what I mean, Pop?"

"Yes I do, Joe. I didn't have that kind of relationship with my dad either. He made a lot of mistakes, failed, and disappointed me too. My father's gone now. He died twenty years ago. I can't do anything about the kind of father *he* was, but I can do something about the kind of father *I* am. Just like you can do something about the kind of son you are. It means being a man like Louise Dodd's father was—a man of integrity."

"So, Pop, how did Father's Day become a legal holiday?"

"Louise Dodd persuaded her church to salute fathers with a special service, and in 1910, the first Father's Day was celebrated. President Woodrow Wilson officially approved the idea in 1916. Then, in 1924 President Calvin Coolidge recommended that the nation observe the occasion. It wasn't until 1972, though, that President Nixon signed it into law. Did you know the red and white rose is recognized as the official Father's Day flower?"

"No, but it explains why my sister sends red roses to my father every Father's Day."

"How's your father doing, Joe?"

"I don't know. We're not communicating."

"Why not?"

"I gave my father everything I owned when I came to prison," Joe responded. "All I asked was for him to look out for me while I was in prison. I've only received one letter from him and that was to tell me my dog died."

"Father's Day is a day that we take time out to honor our fathers. The fifth commandment says to honor your father and mother. It doesn't say to honor them only if they're good and they don't make mistakes or disappoint us. It says to honor them, period. It's the only commandment with a promise."

"What promise is that, Pop?"

"That you'll live a long life."

"It says that?"

"Yes, it's right here in Exodus chapter 20, verse 12." Pointing to the passage in his Bible, Pop read, "Honor thy father and thy mother: that thy days may be long upon the land which the LORD thy God giveth thee."

"Do you have any children?"

"Yes, I have a daughter, but she's a lot like you," Pop replied. "She isn't communicating with me. I haven't heard from her in years, but I haven't given up. I know God will reach her when the time is right."

"What's her name?"

"Rita. You know, Joe, I'll bet your father feels the same way about you that I do about Rita."

"You think so?"

"Absolutely. You say you wish you had a father like Louise Dodd had? Well, how about instead say, 'I want to be a father like that'?"

"How do I do that, Pop? I don't have children."

"By doing what Louise Dodd said that her father did—follow God with your actions not just your words; be a man of integrity. You say you want to be valued for who you are. Well, Joe, how about valuing your father for who he is?"

"You make a lot of sense. Hey, do you have any pictures of Rita?"

"Yeah, I got a couple. Why?"

"May I see them?"

"Hey, Joe. What you in here for?"

"Come on, you know I'm in here for burglary."

"Yeah, I know." Pop laughed and pulled the pictures out of his locker.

As Joe looked through the photos, he asked, "How long since you've seen her?"

"About twenty years. The last I heard she's still living in Florida with her three children. She's divorced and raising them herself."

"Maybe she'll send you a Father's Day card this year, Pop."

"I doubt it, Joe. She's never sent me one before, but you never know."

"I'm going to pray for God to touch her heart."

"Thanks, Joe, but I want you to pray that God will restore the relationship with your father."

Joe stood up and shook Pop's hand. "I will. I promise." As Joe headed to the handball court, he passed a telephone. He stopped and made a call.

"Hi, sis."

"Hi Joe. I was just talking about you."

"You were? With whom?"

"Dad."

"Oh yeah? What did he have to say?"

"He just wanted to know how you were doing," his sister replied.

"That's nice. It's good to know he cares. Actually, I was just talking about Dad with my roommate, Pop. We were discussing Father's Day and how special it is."

"Why don't you send Dad a Father's Day card?"

"I was thinking about doing just that, sis. It's not too late for us to have a meaningful relationship. Like my roomie says, 'We all make mistakes.' Hey, can you do me a favor?"

"What?"

"Please send a Father's Day card to my roomie, Pop, and sign it 'Rita.' It would make his day. I owe him for making me see Dad from a different perspective. I'll call you back soon. I love you."

On Friday, June 15, Joe said, "Well, Pop, today's the last day to receive mail before Father's Day."

"I'm not expecting anything, Joe."

"I sent my dad a Father's Day card."

"You did?"

"Yeah! After our talk the other day I realized you were

right. If I want my father to value me for who I am, I need to value him for who he is. I want to walk the talk and become a man of integrity."

As they talked, the mailman walked over and handed each of them an envelope.

"What you got there?" Joe inquired as he watched Pop stare silently at the letter.

Pop's hands trembled. "I'm scared to open it. My daughter's name is on the return address, but I don't recognize the handwriting on the envelope."

"Well, aren't you going to open it?" Joe asked impatiently.

"Who wrote to *you*?"

"My sister. She's coming to see me on Father's Day. She said Dad received the card and was pleased."

"Wow! That's great, Joe."

"Yeah, now it's your turn. Open it!"

Pop tore into the envelope. As he read, tears rolled down his cheeks. In the middle of the card was a crimson rose made from a folded paper napkin. He held it up, and showed it to Joe. Wiping away tears he said, "I taught her how to make these years ago. I had no idea she remembered. I didn't tell you, but since we talked the other day, I've been praying every night, asking God to restore your relationship with your father and mine with Rita. This is His answer. We have an awesome God, Joe."

Joe hugged Pop and went to call his sister to thank her for sending the card. "Thanks, sis. Pop loved it, especially the rose."

"What rose?"

"The rose you sent in the card."

"I never sent it, Joe," his sister confessed. "I didn't think it was a good idea."

"Oh my! That means Pop really got a card and red paper rose from his daughter."

"Wonderful! Pop's prayer wasn't the only prayer that was answered, Joe. Dad is coming to visit you on Sunday—with me."

"That's incredible! He does answer our prayers. Pop's right. We do have an awesome God."

Returning to his cell, Joe found Pop ready to go out to the yard. "Where are you going?"

Pop wrapped his arm around Joe's shoulder. "I'm taking you to the handball court. When I'm done whipping you, you're going to swear I'm twenty-something." They laughed as they walked out to the yard.

❧

It's always good to have a strong bond with your family. No matter how much you may think they don't care about you, chances are, you're wrong. I, unfortunately, had to find this out the hard way.

Brian M. Fisher

THE IN SIDE by Matt Matteo

Reprinted by permission of Matt Matteo and Tom Lagana.

It took coming to prison for me to realize that everything I had been looking for in life, I already had.

Dale Gaudet

Connect with Family: Cherish and Nurture the Gift of Love

TOM LAGANA AND LAURA LAGANA

2.1 Who do you love?

2.2 When was the last time you said to them or wrote, "I love you"? Take action and remind them that you love them. When you can be sincere about it, finish every phone call, conclude your visits, and sign off each letter with the words, "I love you."

2.3 When you write a letter, reread it and ask yourself, *Is this really what I want to say? Did I say something negative that I could have stated in a more positive way?*

2.4 Pray for the person to whom you are writing. Hold the letter between your palms, close your eyes, and fill it with your mental prayers and good wishes. (Editor's note: As we write this, we are praying for you.)

2.5 If you knew you would die in three days and were allowed only two phone calls, who would you call and what would you say? What single message would you want each person to remember as your last words to them?

THREE

Liberating Forgiveness

As a prison chaplain, I hung my Pardon Document
on my office wall to inform all who entered that
a willingness to provide a second chance and
forgiveness are part of the humanity of our society.

ROD CARTER

The Real Heroes

DALE GAUDET

Not long ago, I spoke to a group of high school students and parents about the effects prison life has on the entire family. I went on to tell the group about the day my two young daughters came to visit me when I came to prison fourteen years ago.

Our noncontact visit behind a glass wall was so noisy from other visitors around us that we were unable to hear each another. My daughter, Stacy, inched her way toward the glass and placed the open palm of her hand against it. This simple gesture of love melted my heart in a way that only a child could convey. This story became known as "The Healing Touch" in *Chicken Soup for the Prisoner's Soul*. But the story doesn't end there.

I went on to tell the group that my daughter is now married with a family of her own and that her life has been a struggle due to my being in prison. It's often said that a picture is worth a thousand words.

I looked out at the parents in the audience. As I held up a drawing of two small handprints and a red heart bearing the words "We Love You, Paw Paw," I concluded my presentation with "Fourteen years ago, her mother's hand gave me the strength and courage to endure. Today, my granddaughter, Chloe, offers her hands as a sign of love and support."

There wasn't a dry eye in the house, but the real impact of the message came when a parent came up to me and gave me a hug. He explained, "I resented coming here with my daughter on this field trip today. To be honest, I have no compassion for anyone who breaks the law, but seeing Chloe's drawings gave me new insight. Please forgive me. I never thought of a prisoner as a dad or a grandfather!"

I have come to live with this life sentence each and every day. I have accepted my fate and punishment, but no amount of time is equal to the anguish I have caused my family or that of my victim's family. In that moment, I gave someone a chance to see how unwavering and unconditional the love of a young child is, even in dire circumstances.

I'm very proud of my family. They are the real heroes who look beyond my faults and weaknesses—and can still say, "We love you, Paw Paw!"

THE IN SIDE by Matt Matteo

Reprinted by permission of Matt Matteo.

An Unlikely Path to Forgiveness

LAURA LAGANA

As the doctor walked into the recovery room, the awful words poured from Kelly's mouth, "That's impossible. I talked to Nancy just a few hours ago."

Standing there, in the same hospital where Kelly had given birth to her precious Nancy seventeen years earlier, all the doctor could say was, "I'm terribly sorry."

Nothing more could be said. Nothing could bring Nancy back. Kelly's daughter lay dead on the operating room table next door. She had been stabbed to death by an acquaintance, Leon, a sixteen-year-old young man.

One year later, Kelly learned that they had been fighting over drugs when Leon picked up a knife from the kitchen counter. From that moment on, nothing in this distraught mother's life would ever be the same again.

Kelly put her trust and faith in God, knowing He would use this incident for His purpose. She has forgiven Leon for the murder of her daughter. She could have remained angry and devastated forever, but God has helped her find ways to touch others through her own pain and loss.

Thirteen years ago, Kelly began volunteering in the prison system. This may seem an unlikely place to find someone whose only child has been murdered, but that is where she finds peace and joy. Many prisoners have lost hope and don't know what it's like to have someone care about them. When Kelly talks to inmates, she feels her daughter's presence deep in her heart and soul.

While conducting a Prison Fellowship Bible study, Kelly met Jay, who was serving a life sentence for the murder of his girlfriend twenty years before. The discussion in the group that evening focused on forgiveness. Kelly shared about how she had forgiven Leon. After class, Jay waited until almost everyone was gone before approaching her. "Someday I want to be able to tell the parents of the girl I murdered that I'm deeply sorry," he said. Jay also shared his remorse and how his life changed over the years.

Kelly worked with Jay for more than a year before she attended a pardon hearing on his behalf. The memory of that day will live in her heart forever. The victim's parents and Jay's adult daughter sat in the front row of a small courtroom. Kelly sat several rows behind. Although she couldn't see their faces, she could feel their pain by the way they sat, shoulders bent forward and heads bowed.

They watched Kelly walk to the lectern, wondering what she would say on behalf of their child's murderer. Kelly saw the unyielding pain in their eyes, along with their intense anger for the man who had caused it. They had not forgiven their daughter's killer. *Any one of them could have been me,* she thought.

When it came time for her to speak, Kelly began, "Our circumstances are similar." After explaining the details, she continued. "Although I can never know your pain, I understand how it feels to lose a child to murder. I have been working with Jay through Prison Fellowship Ministries, and I believe he is a humble man who is truly remorseful for taking your daughter's life. If my daughter's murderer could turn his life around someday, the way Jay has, I would want him to be released."

Jay was not pardoned that day, and he may never be. Although he is aware of this fact, he is hopeful that one day someone will recognize that today he is not the same young man who devastated so many lives. He is now at peace. Jay knows that God has forgiven him, and if someday his victim's family chooses to forgive him, that forgiveness will be the greatest gift he will ever receive.

Kelly feels blessed to have met Jay and all of the inmates she works with as a volunteer in the correctional system. As she readily admits, "I can't imagine what my life would be without them. They have kept me connected to my daughter, but most of all to God—a path I might never have chosen if I hadn't decided to forgive."

[EDITOR'S NOTE: *For information about Prison Fellowship Ministries, contact a prison chaplain or see the website at http://www.prisonfellowship.org.*]

Life is full of choices, and these choices truly determine our destiny. We can choose to lead an honest and productive life, surrounding ourselves with others who do the same, or we can travel down a long and meaningless road of loneliness and despair. It's a choice that only you and I can make. Serving time has taught me the truth of this reality.

Brian M. Fisher

What a Father Feels

JAY ANGELO

My Darling Daughter,

Growing up without my being a significant part of your life, I know you've wondered what I felt about you, so I wanted to share these feelings. I remember the day your mother told me she was pregnant. I had just turned eighteen. The steamy Detroit air was abuzz with the energy of summer. In those first few moments, I felt a rush of conflicting emotions.

After your mother left, I went into the house and sat in the kitchen, thinking about what being a father means. As your cocoa brown fingers and toes were forming inside your mother's womb, thoughts of fatherhood were taking shape inside my young mind. I knew I would love you with everything I had inside of me. To this day I still hold on to that thought.

At the time, I was living outside the boundaries of the law. For the first time in four years, I began to rethink my position. If I was going to be the father that I knew you needed me to be, I would have to give up the street life. The problem was I didn't know how to walk away.

The streets were the one place I felt accepted. Every day and night, up until your birth, I wrestled with myself to make the right decision. As your birth neared, I continued to live the life of desperation on the streets.

With each new month the relationship between your

mother and me ebbed and flowed. Sometimes we got along. We talked about what sharing the responsibility of parenthood was going to be like. At times, we were at each other's throats, and paternity was brought into question.

As a teenager, I wasn't prepared to handle the emotions. I withdrew into myself. I never spoke to anyone about how I felt, not even your mother. I'm telling you today so you'll know what a father feels. I knew in the deepest recesses of my heart that you were my baby girl. You had already claimed a special place inside of me that you'll always occupy.

When your mother brought you home and I held you in my arms for the first time, I felt an eternal bond. Your little smile and twinkling eyes rivaled the stars. Your first cries made me feel protective. I wanted to shield you from the pain and ugliness that life can sometimes bring, but I failed.

Two months later I was hauled off to jail. It was the saddest day of my life, not only because I'd forfeited my freedom but also because I knew I was leaving you behind with so many unanswered questions—one of which I know you must have asked yourself over and over: *What does he feel for me?*

From the beginning of my prison sentence, I sought to connect with you. I knew I couldn't be there physically as a father, but I knew I would be there for you mentally and spiritually, if I were allowed to. Day after day, I prayed for us to be able to know each other as father and daughter. I asked God to bring me into your life. I wanted to be the one man in your life you could count on. I wanted to share your first report card and let you know how proud I was. I wanted to listen to you tell me stories about your first day in school. I wanted to send crumpled dollar bills to your mother for her to place beneath your pillow for the tooth fairy when you lost your baby teeth. I wanted to do all of those things that fathers do for their daughters.

As the years went by, the pain of not being a part of your life threatened to consume me. Something inside told me to hold on because we would have our time together. It is the one thing that has kept me sane even when my heart was breaking. It kept me strong when I was at my weakest point. It kept me focused on our future.

That one special thing I held on to was hope. Every night I hoped the next day would bring me a letter telling me you were okay. I imagined being called out for a visit and finding you standing there by your mother's side. I yearned for a picture of you and maybe even a piece of paper with your scribbling on it. Then one day my hope was answered when I received your first letter.

Today I'm still hopeful that you will grow to understand that I love you. I want to see you reach your full potential as a woman. I've thought about you every day and night since I've been in here. I pray that you will allow me to be a part of your life. But most of all, I hope that you can find it in your heart to forgive me for not being there for the first fifteen years of your life.

We must forgive those we feel have wronged us, not because they deserve to be forgiven, but because we love ourselves so much we don't want to keep paying for the injustice.

Don Miguel Ruiz
author of *The Four Agreements*

The Echo of Tears

KURT R. MOSHER

Last night I heard a teardrop fall
As I lay awake in bed.
It told a story we all know
But keep inside our head.

It talked of faded laughter,
And dreams that won't come true.
It reminisced about childhood days,
And things we used to do.

It talked of love that's long since gone,
And love that might have grown.
It spoke of things we would have done,
If we had only known.

It remembered the taste of birthday cake,
And the smell of Christmas trees;
It recalled the ocean to a boy
That as a man he'll never see.

But in the dark, the last sound heard
Still echoes in my ears:
And that is the sound a prison cell makes
When it's filling up with tears.

*Being incarcerated takes away some of the thrill of
Christmas, but nothing can ever take away the majestic
miracle of our Lord's birth.*

B. L. Scott

Becoming Brutally Honest

DOUGLAS BURGESS

Today included one of those humbling moments that reminded me of the purpose for which I've been created. On Wednesday nights, I attend Christian group counseling. With twenty or more fellow inmates, the discussions can become brutally honest, such as during our talk about regret. I dug down deep to explain the conflicted emotions relating to my dad.

On the one hand he was my dad, and for that and his good days, I loved him. But then there was that rough side of him, who didn't flinch from lashing out verbally or physically. During this discussion, I spoke about my personal demons as a means of exorcising them from my nightmares.

The next day on the yard, Tony asked to speak to me. The guy fell apart on me, crying and confessing how, in his alcoholic state, he used to do the same things to his son that I had experienced from my dad. To say I was more than a bit taken aback is an understatement.

After a lot of talking in the frigid air, Tony literally begged me to help him make amends with his family. I was stunned. I mean, I'm not prepared for this sort of thing, but I agreed to type his letters to his wife and son.

As I typed Tony's personal letter to his son, it was a good thing both of my bunkmates were out of our room. I found it difficult to keep a dry eye. The pure, raw emotion Tony choked out yanked me back thirty years. I yearned to hear such words from my own father. I don't know which of us gained more, but I'm grateful for the blessing of this encounter with Tony.

❧ ❧

THE IN SIDE by Matt Matteo

Reprinted by permission of Matt Matteo.

Afraid to Forgive

KARL B. STRUNK

People often inquire as to whether I have forgiven myself for taking a life some twenty years ago. For those who appear genuinely interested, my response regularly consists of the ensuing discourse.

What does it mean to forgive? Ideally, forgiveness encompasses a willingness to abandon resentment or the desire for retribution toward a wrongdoer. Unfortunately, our current cultural use of the term "forgiveness" has become trite, cast about carelessly like the phrase, "I love you."

Reduced to little more than a cliché, for those who indeed appreciate the literal meaning of forgiveness, I would seemingly come across as callous or pretentious if I claimed to have absolved my anguish. In this regard, I likewise agree. Why? Because I feel that forgiving myself would be tantamount to saying that taking a life was somehow acceptable. Irrespective of the victim being my father, which is an additional grief in itself, this is in all conscience the most serious of offenses.

The very moment I ended my father's life, there was an immediate and crushing realization of what I had done. Even today, I close my eyes and shake my head in disbelief at the sheer senselessness of it all. For perspective, take a moment and remember what it felt like when somebody close to you passed away and how sick, hurt, and helpless you felt. Now imagine that you were the one who caused that death. I experience the magnitude of those feelings every day. There is no outrunning them. My feelings are further compounded by the awareness that I caused other people, my family, and a whole community to feel the same.

Whenever I reminisce about my adolescence or contemplate the future, each thought is punctuated with that last fleeting moment in my father's life. Distressful as this may seem, I am afraid that if I were to somehow forgive myself, memory of this heinous action would fade, essentially reducing the tragedy to nothing. There is also a phobia that I would lose all recollection of my father, his strong physical features, his German accent, the distinct apple aroma of his pipe tobacco, the way he would sometimes nap at the kitchenette, and the father-son fishing trips—neither one of us could catch a fish unless by accident, but it was time we spent together. My father did not have the opportunity to see how I have matured, the way I have utilized the gems of his parental guidance, or my accomplishments. I was a confused mess of anger and turmoil when he last saw me, unable to find my way. He will never have the peace of knowing that I am all right, that I eventually made it through my struggles.

For all intents and purposes, this is my penance, albeit self-imposed. Without doubt, incarceration is an inhospitable existence and such has proven to be a quandary of epic proportions. I love my father and miss him dearly. Though nothing can be done to alleviate what happened, I can ensure the seriousness of this is never lessened. To do otherwise would be a further insult to my father.

When prisoners seek forgiveness and victims struggle to redeem the past, harmony can return to a broken community, even after a great loss or tragedy. It's called restorative justice.

Rod Carter

Forgiving the Person I Hated the Most
TOM LAGANA

Almost everyone I meet receives a hug—a hug coupon, that is. My unique calling cards not only provide information about our business but are also redeemable for a hug, a smile, or an act of kindness.

Working with inmates doesn't make me the most sought-after member of social circles, but it does provide an element of interest when I meet people. Other people's opinions of me don't ruffle my feathers. Some folks have asked blunt questions like, "You work with prisoners? Why do you stoop so low?" Whenever I hear such comments from uninformed people, I look them in the eyes and think to myself, *I'd rather be chatting with an inmate than listening to you right now.* Most people are receptive to our work; for them the hug coupons are a constructive icebreaker.

On a trip to Arizona, my wife and I took several tours, including Sedona's energy vortexes, the Grand Canyon, and the Hopi Indian reservation. Each tour lasted most of the day, giving us an opportunity to get to know the handful of people who shared the experience with us. Two of our guides were Native Americans who helped pass the time during our long drives by describing tribal customs and sharing native folklore.

I gave everyone a hug coupon during our excursions. When our crew realized the connection my wife and I have with prisoners, they revealed aspects of their private lives that under other circumstances would have remained private.

The guide on our first excursion told us about his son who was serving a long prison sentence. A Canadian gentleman seated behind us in the van mentioned that after a gratifying twenty-year career in corrections, he now ministers to inmates.

On the final tour, our Native American guide, George, mentioned that he had been incarcerated. As the hours unfolded, he revealed more about himself, along with local and ancestral history. He seemed almost relieved to be able to talk about what had happened to him years before. He had worked hard to become a successful guide and expert in his field.

Near the end of our adventure, I felt compelled to ask, "What made you turn your life around?"

"One day it hit me. I realized if I wanted to change my life, I needed to forgive the person I hated the most."

"Who was that?" I asked. Conversation ceased as we focused on what George would say next.

"It wasn't my mother or father or anyone who'd harmed me. The person I hated the most was the person I faced every morning when I shaved. Every day in prison, when I looked in the mirror, I realized I hated myself. Deep inside my heart, I knew I had to do something about it."

We waited patiently for George to continue. "Each day I'd look in the mirror and say to myself, *I forgive you, and I love you*. It felt phony at first. I didn't believe it, but I felt the need to say it every day. One day I finally accepted the idea that I'm a worthwhile person who deserves to be forgiven."

As we stepped out of the van, we all redeemed our hug coupons. I think we realized that a loving Spirit in a mystical land had touched us in a unique way, allowing us to make a special connection.

Beyond Your Outdate

CARLA WILSON

As a correctional officer in a county jail, I felt that I was in a position to do more than just supervise the men and women by providing some type of psychological relief and inspiration.

One morning at the beginning of my shift, I glanced around the unit, noticing the eyes of many men filled with despair. Observing that words of encouragement seemed to uplift their mood and demeanor, I asked them to sit in a group so I could share a few short stories. Most of the stories had down-to-earth messages, showing that anything is possible, based on the choices we make. Messages like these are empowering.

As I experimented, I learned that guided meditation helped them make changes in their lives. Ultimately they learned they can control their actions by controlling their thoughts. Here is an example of a guided meditation that I facilitate in the units I supervise:

Beyond Your Outdate—A Guided Meditation

Today we will begin by looking at the desires of your heart. What is it that you really want for yourself beyond your outdate? Today I want you to challenge yourself to look deep within for new answers and for new truths. I want you to tap into the power of your mind. Your mind is more sophisticated than any computer ever made. It is important that you do not limit yourself in your choices. Remember to think BIG, because all of your answers lie within you.

Let's begin by taking a very deep, cleansing breath, and then slowly exhale.

When you think of your future, what is it that you really want? Close your eyes and begin seeing yourself doing whatever it is you want to do. Where do you want to be? What do you see yourself doing? Who is around you? What are the desires of your heart? Let's begin by unlocking the door to your future.

Take another deep breath. Inhale as deeply as you can, and then slowly exhale.

Imagine yourself placing your hand on a doorknob and turning it. Whatever true happiness looks and feels like for you, take a step toward that vision and begin to look around. Whether it is driving a new vehicle, starting a business, returning to school, building a home, or returning to a familiar relationship, take a look around and take in what you see and feel. Is there anyone with you? Look for colors and textures. Notice how you feel. When images begin to appear, observe them. Accept them, and enjoy the moment. Let your mind and body relax as you continue to walk around your life and explore your future.

Slowly begin looking at yourself from the outside. What are you wearing? How do you know that it's you? Continue walking around your world that you have created. Start looking for details, and realize that it's possible. Don't worry about how it will all take place. Take in everything that your mind has allowed you to visualize, and be grateful. These are the things that can occur when you don't limit yourself.

Continue to look around and make the connection. Take another deep breath and slowly exhale.

Everything that has happened in your life has happened for a reason . . . the good and the bad. Your pain has been a preparation for your destiny. It's time to recognize these lessons and move forward. It's time to let go of resentments, shame, guilt, or any emotion that keeps you stuck. It's time to move forward with open arms and happiness because you have arrived. You no longer have to be in a survival mode, because you have arrived and you deserve the best.

Take one more look before your scene goes to darkness. Know that you are worthy and that you are capable of having all of your dreams come true. Allow your view to go into darkness for now. Then open your eyes.

꒰ ꒱

Go to your place of quiet and safety. Relax your body and visualize it as filled with light blurred by globs of darkness. The dark spots are the shadows of unforgiven offenses against you. When memories resurface, they swell and possess your thoughts, crippling your emotions and ultimately affecting your physical health. Examine the shadows to identify any that might be self-inflicted, such as through an addiction or deceitfulness. Relive those instances. What motivated you to harm yourself? Consider how you can convert these behaviors and talents for the good of yourself and others. Visualize the negative energy and debris dropping from the globs, now becoming light, as you forgive yourself.

Lois McGinnis
author of *The Way to Your True Self*

The Prison Yogi

DAN MILLSTEIN

One hot summer day one of our students, Nick, was practicing yoga in the exercise yard. As he stretched into a different pose, the razor wire seemed to disappear for a brief moment. An abrupt, "Hey, you there. Get your shoes on," broke his reverie. Nick looked straight up into the face of a young correctional officer he hadn't seen before.

"Sorry, officer. Were you speaking to me?"

"Yeah, you're the only one around here with his shoes off, aren't you?"

There's no particular rule on the books about having to wear shoes when exercising, but anything is fair game in prison.

Nick explained to the officer, "This is part of my religious practice, sir. I've been doing yoga in the yard, in this very spot, for many years, and I've never been notified that I'm breaking any rule." He stopped short of mentioning the fact that only days before, the warden had come by and stopped to converse with a group of men practicing yoga together.

"Rules are rules. Now go on, and put your shoes back on," the unimpressed officer retorted.

Seeing the futility in pursuing the matter further and having no particular need to be right, a universal trait of good yogis, Nick complied with the order.

As he began to tie his shoelaces, the officer asked, "What kind of religion is stretching?" Before Nick could formulate an answer, the young officer added, "Could that stuff help my back?"

Suddenly, an energy shift occurred. The officer became a student, and Nick became a teacher. For more than an hour, Nick gave him a caring explanation of yoga and also included a detailed demonstration of postures that would be helpful for anyone plagued by chronic back pain. They were no longer adversaries.

Weeks later, Nick was practicing postures in the yard without shoes. He was joined by a group of other prisoners practicing in unison. The same young officer strolled over to report, "My back is much better. I can deal with the pain now. I feel like a changed man. My family life has improved, and I enjoy playing with my little boy again, thanks to you."

THE IN SIDE by Matt Matteo

Reprinted by permission of Matt Matteo.

Make Repairs: Forgive Yourself, Forgive Others, Make Amends

TOM LAGANA AND LAURA LAGANA

Forgive yourself and others. Making amends also means to apologize, ask for forgiveness, say you're sorry, or express regret.

3.1 Who do you need to forgive?

3.2 Who do you need to ask to forgive you?

3.3 List everyone who falls into this category. Contact each person and ask, "Will you forgive me?" or say, "I forgive you."

3.4 Look at yourself in the mirror and stare into your eyes. Talk to your reflection. Tell yourself what you're feeling. (Example: "I'm proud of you for . . ." and "I forgive you for . . .") Once you've shared your feelings with the inner you, conclude with, "And, I love you."

3.5 What do you need to forgive *yourself* for?

3.6 If you had all the time, money, and resources you wanted, how would you repair the damage that you did to the person or people you have wronged, mistreated, or offended? Write an action plan.

3.7 In private, repeat each of the following phrases to yourself six times: I forgive everyone who has ever done anything to me at any time.
I am sorry for everything that I have ever done to anyone at any time, and I am forgiven.

FOUR

Compassion in Action

We may be incarcerated, but we are still human beings, longing for acceptance, attention, and love. A simple facial gesture, such as a smile, can truly make a prisoner's day. Judge us not for the mistakes we made, but give light and hope so that one day we may become productive individuals in society.

MARK T. PIECZYNSKI

Nurse Bonnie

KEN "DUKE" MONSE'BROTEN

As far as I know, everybody just called her Bonnie. I can't recall her last name, but she was truly one in a million. Bonnie was a nurse on the second floor of the hospital in Washington State Penitentiary in Walla Walla, Washington, around 1971. She was one of those hands-on people. Whenever Bonnie talked to an inmate, she had her hand on his arm or shoulder, or she would straighten his collar. She always had time to talk to everyone—and she could talk! We all loved her, and it was very evident that she truly cared for us.

A big former heavyweight boxer named Elmer was doing time with the rest of us. He had been shot in the forehead by a police officer. The bullet split when it hit Elmer, and it reduced him to the mentality of an eight-year-old, even though he was a giant of a man. The bullet caused such damage to Elmer's brain that he forgot how to read or write, and it also caused him to have terrible headaches when he forgot to take his medication.

These headaches often put Elmer into screaming rages. When these rages happened, the Goon Squad was called, and he was taken to the hospital by force for his medication. The one thing Elmer never forgot was how to fight. He would put several of these specially trained guards on the injured list every time they had to subdue him.

I was working in the prison hospital one day when Bonnie came to my work area. She was leading a bashful Elmer by the hand. "Duke, have you met my friend Elmer?" she asked. I knew enough about Elmer to stay as far away from him as possible. It was a well-known fact that there weren't any two convicts in the place who could whip Elmer. I said that I knew him and hoped it would end there. He scared me, and everyone was afraid of Elmer—except Bonnie.

"Well," she said with a wink. "Elmer has a problem. He lost his glasses so he can't read or write very well. He has a letter from his daughter that he has been carrying around in his pocket for more than a month, but he's too bashful to ask anyone to read it for him. I want you to read the letter to him, Duke, and help him answer it. Will you do that for me?"

What could I say? The poor guy was ashamed of not being able to read, so I read the letter to him. It was from his daughter, and she had recently had a baby. She wanted to know if Elmer wished to see some pictures of his grandson. She also wanted him to arrange things so she could come and visit. It had been almost thirteen years since she had seen her father.

When I finished reading the letter to Elmer, Bonnie started making a big fuss over it. "Elmer, you are a grandpa! Do you know that?"

Elmer smiled, his head wobbling from side to side. The scene was one for the books. This tiny nurse was bouncing around this huge, unpredictable convict. Bonnie was so happy she was just vibrating with joy and pinching Elmer's cheek as she teased.

After Bonnie left, Elmer and I started to answer the letter. Elmer leaned over to me and said in a low voice, "Maybe ya can read it 'gain ta me 'cause I don't hear too good neither."

I read the letter to him again and again. After each reading, Elmer would ask questions like, "How do ta baby know I'm his grandpa? Do ya think ta baby gonna like me?" After countless readings and questions, we finally answered the letter and enclosed a visiting form for his daughter.

In the weeks that followed, Elmer would bring any new letters he got to Bonnie, who would, in turn, bring him back to my work area. I really looked forward to helping him with his letters. I also discovered his gentle side—a side that Bonnie was quick to see.

One day, while Elmer and I were working on one of his letters, Bonnie came in and sat down. After listening to us for a few minutes she asked, "Elmer, if you could have anything you wanted in here, what would it be?"

"Oh, nothing," Elmer answered bashfully. "I'm okay."

"There must be something you would like, Elmer," Bonnie persisted. "You think about it and tell me three things that would make you happier here."

A few days later Elmer came up to me in the prison yard. He told me if he could have anything, it would be to watch morning cartoons on the television, have a job like the other convicts, and get some Tootsie Rolls. I related his wishes to Bonnie.

Bonnie went to the watch commander and talked him into giving Elmer the job of cleaning the television room on weekends. The Tootsie Rolls weren't sold in the inmates' store, so Bonnie would bring in a few for him every day she worked.

Elmer did his job well. He had his own mop and bucket locked in the janitor's closet. He was proud, and you might be surprised to see how clean the convicts kept things when they knew they had to answer to Elmer for any mess they failed to clean up.

Bonnie and I noticed that whenever either one of us had to go somewhere in the prison, Elmer followed. We were both teased about having a full-time bodyguard. Elmer was making sure no one messed with his letter writer and Tootsie Roll connection.

One day Bonnie heard, over the guard's radio, that Elmer was going berserk with another headache in Wing 4. The Goon Squad was called and the hospital alerted for possible injuries. Bonnie immediately ran to Wing 4, ahead of the others, to confront Elmer. She walked up to the front of his cell with a stern look on her face, scolding the raving giant, much like a parent would scold a young child who had misbehaved.

"Elmer, you just quit this and come over to the hospital with me right now! This is foolish; and if you don't settle down, I'm never going to give you another Tootsie Roll." Bonnie certainly told Elmer, and by the time help arrived, she and her Tootsie Roll bodyguard were already walking out.

Years later I came through the prison at Walla Walla once again. Bonnie was still there but about to leave for retirement. She had had numerous changes in her life. Her husband had died and her daughters were grown with families of their own. We talked for a while, and when it came time for her to go, I asked, "Bonnie, have you run into any more Tootsie Roll bodyguards lately?"

For the first time since I'd known Bonnie, she was lost for words. She stared out the window and after a few moments of silence looked back at me. With tears in her eyes she said, "Wasn't he a little sweetheart?" Bonnie went on to tell me about how Elmer died in the late 1970s, a delayed result of the gunshot wound.

Nurse Bonnie was one in a million, and she truly cared, no matter who was hurt or hurting, whether we were convicts or not.

❧ ❧

As a correctional officer at roll call, I frequently attempt to tell each inmate who they are, before they show me their wristbands. When they know that I have taken a personal interest to learn who they are, it adds to an overall sense of community.

Carla Wilson

Christmas Angel

CHARLES CARKHUFF

As Christmas approached, a dark cloud of depression, guilt, and shame hung over the prison. The loneliness I saw on the faces of the other inmates reflected my own feelings of isolation on what should have been a festive occasion.

The tiny fake Christmas tree standing alone in the corner of the dayroom was a cruel reminder that life on the outside had no place for the incarcerated. Even the true meaning of Christmas evaded me as I watched the snow falling silently to the ground.

Knowing that I had no one to blame except myself for my situation did little to console me. The person in my family who was affected the most, my elderly mother, lived too far away to visit. She and I were very close. My predicament was extremely difficult for both of us to bear.

I tried in vain to block the nagging thoughts of my mother, sitting alone in her small apartment with no visitors, without a tree, presents, or holiday dinner. Because of my absence, she abandoned any hope of celebrating Christmas. I'd often heard Christmas referred to as a magical time of year, a time of blessings and wonder, but I didn't believe anything could penetrate the cold prison walls that year.

Shortly before Christmas, I received a letter from a prison volunteer who had sent me a Bible correspondence course years earlier. Though we had become pen pal friends, I was totally unprepared for what Kathleen wrote in her letter. She asked if she could send a few gifts to my mother. Although they had never met, I had written a lot about my mother in all the letters I sent to Kathleen. This kind lady wrote, "I'll put your name on the gift tags."

Tears of happiness stung my eyes at this outpouring of unconditional love. I humbly and gratefully accepted her generous offer of kindness. Even though my mother and I were hundreds of miles apart, it seemed like we would somehow be closer now. The dim lights surrounding the prison yard suddenly seemed to take on a festive appearance. Snow glistened off the razor wire like stars in the heavens. Although I was unable to call my mother that Christmas, I had a new peace in my heart, because I felt that an angel watched over us.

A few days after Christmas, when I was able to call home, my mother cried when she heard my voice. Through her tears of joy she asked, "Son, how were you able to arrange for such wonderful presents to arrive on Christmas Eve?" Sounding like a child on Christmas morning, she marveled over her beautifully wrapped gifts, describing each one in great detail.

In our darkest of days, a compassionate volunteer became our Christmas angel who touched the hearts of two lonely people in desperate need of kindness. This small miracle changed the way I view the sad events of my life. Not even concrete walls and bars can stop a mission of love.

❧ ❧

Constant kindness can accomplish much. As the sun makes ice melt, kindness causes misunderstanding, mistrust, and hostility to evaporate.

Dr. Albert Schweitzer

Entertaining Angels

JAYE LEWIS

It was fifty years ago on a hot summer day in the Deep South.

We lived on a dirt road, on a sand lot. We were what was known as "dirt poor."

I had been playing outside all morning in the sand. Suddenly, I heard a sharp clanking sound behind me, and looking over my shoulder, my eyes were drawn to a strange sight!

Across the dirt road were two rows of men dressed in black-and-white striped, baggy uniforms. Their faces were covered with dust and sweat. They looked so weary, and they were chained together with huge, black, iron chains. Hanging from the end of each chained row was a big black iron ball. They were, as polite people said in those days, a "chain gang," guarded by two heavily armed guards.

I stared at the prisoners as they settled uncomfortably down in the dirt, under the shade of some straggly trees.

One of the guards walked toward me.

Nodding as he passed, he went up to our front door and knocked. My mother appeared at the door, and I heard the guard ask if he could have permission to get water from the pump in the backyard so that "his men" could "have a drink." My mother agreed, but I saw a look of concern on her face as she called me inside.

I stared through the window as each prisoner was unchained

from the line to hobble over to the pump and drink his fill from a small tin cup, while a guard watched vigilantly. It wasn't long before they were all chained up again, with prisoners and guards retreating into the shade away from an unrelenting sun.

I heard my mother call me into the kitchen, and I entered to see her bustling around with tins of tuna fish, mayonnaise, our last loaf of bread, and two big pitchers of lemonade. In what seemed a blink of an eye, she had made a tray of sandwiches using all the tuna we were to have had for that night's supper.

My mother was smiling as she handed me one of the pitchers of lemonade, cautioning me to carry it "carefully" and to "not spill a drop." Then, lifting the tray in one hand and holding a pitcher in her other hand, she marched me to the door, deftly opening it with her foot, and trotted me across the street.

She approached the guards, flashing them a brilliant smile. "We had some leftovers from lunch," she said, "and I was wondering if we could share with you and your men." She smiled at each of the men, searching their dark eyes with her own eyes of robin's egg blue. Everyone started to their feet. "Oh no!" she said. "Stay where you are! I'll just serve you!"

Calling me to her side, she went from guard to guard, then from prisoner to prisoner—filling each tin cup with lemonade, and giving each man a sandwich. It was very quiet, except for a "thank you, ma'am," and the clanking of the chains. Very soon we were at the end of the line, my mother's eyes softly scanning each face.

The last prisoner was a big man, his dark skin pouring with sweat and streaked with dust. Suddenly, his face broke into a wonderful smile as he looked up into my mother's eyes, and he said, "Ma'am, I've wondered all my life if I'd ever see an angel, and now I have! Thank you!"

Again, my mother's smile took in the whole group. "You're all welcome!" she said. "God bless you." Then we walked across to the house, with empty tray and pitchers, and back inside. Soon, the men moved on, and I never saw them again.

The only explanation my mother ever gave me for that strange and wonderful day was to "remember, always, to entertain strangers, for by doing so, you may be entertaining angels, without knowing." Then, with a mysterious smile, she went about the rest of the day.

I don't remember what we ate for supper that night. I just know it was served by an angel.

My problems were so deep within me, I needed a heart transplant, and that could only come from God. So, during my incarceration, I stayed by myself and concentrated on Him. I read the Bible every day and prayed every moment possible. I needed help beyond what any man could give, so I talked to God.

Brian Brookheart
author of *A Prisoner: Released*
and *The Ten Best Days of My Life*

Blinded by the Light

JAMES GUY

In the dreariness of a cold, winter evening confined in prison, the thought of a special guest at Bible study brought us all to a heightened sense of expectation. During these past fourteen months, we'd heard about and prayed for a young woman named Sharon, the married daughter of Tom and Darlyne. This kindhearted couple conducted our Bible study class.

We prayed for Sharon while listening to reports of her struggle with the treatments for liver cancer. We heard of her emotional battle with this horrible disease and the strife of her family, husband, and children. All of us witnessed the pain and anxiety her parents were experiencing, seeing their daughter and loved ones struggle.

Each one of us held the great hope that the Lord would intervene and provide their daughter with the gift of time to raise her young family. We joined hands and prayed together for her recovery. We wrote cards of encouragement and then returned to our cells during the week, where we continued our prayers. Their struggle took our minds off of our own plight.

By November, during the lowest point of Sharon's prognosis, she and her family took a trip to Myrtle Beach, South Carolina. At this point, we understood that Sharon would not live much longer. In spite of our faith and hope in our Lord, we could not help but question, *Why? Why does God take a faithful child, a kindhearted mother and servant to others? What possible motive does God possess to take her from her family, children, and loved ones?* In spite of our questions, we prayed as our hearts felt the strain. Yet Sharon came to visit *us*, some of the most undeserving citizens on earth.

Entering through the door of the chapel, I was overcome with emotion as I saw the tiny, emaciated body of a frail, gentle woman sitting off to the side in a wheelchair. Standing tall beside her was her husband. I couldn't help but reflect on the confusion and frustration her husband must be feeling over her insistence to be with us this evening. She could be at home sharing her last moments with her children. Some of our own family members didn't even visit us. What motivated Sharon to be with us this evening?

I walked over to her. Not knowing what to do or say, I extended a hand and enclosed hers in mine. I looked into a jaundiced face with sunken eyes. A beautiful smile spread across her face, as if she understood my struggle to find words that could adequately express my feelings. I could barely manage to whisper, "God bless you." Each person after me seemed to suffer the same difficulty of not knowing what to say. As the Bible study continued, her proud father gave Sharon a loving glance, while her mother, Darlyne, tried to hide her tears.

Then Sharon stood up and was helped over to the piano. She played hymns and Christmas carols. Soon we were all fighting back tears. I wondered, *How can she keep herself together during this emotion-packed moment?*

After several more hymns, she was assisted back to her wheelchair. Again, her devoted husband stood beside her, holding her hand. Most of us in the sanctuary were fighting off tears, and yet Sharon and her husband seemed unfazed. *Why her, Lord? None of this makes sense.*

In the most agonizing of these moments, a mysterious light shone in my soul. I sprung up from the pew, walked to the front of the chapel, and paused for a second to gaze at the beautiful woman in the wheelchair before I told her, and everyone present, what I thought God was telling us.

"Sometimes we get upset and feel sorry for ourselves. We focus on our own problems and become lost in misery. We forget about others and dwell on ourselves. We feel forgotten and lost. In our abandonment, we don't believe God cares enough for us, and we feel overlooked by Him, especially during the holidays. Well, this year God has granted us a gift: a Christian heroine who has come to us during her darkest hour. She comes, not in pain, suffering, or self-indulgence, but with love, caring, and compassion.

"God is showing us the power and glory of His unconditional love. Other than the gift of His Son, I can think of no greater love. Sharon's strength overcomes every selfish concern and thought. She shines brightly as God's example of His power, love, and compassion. She is our heroine. In her time of need, He blesses us with this awesome demonstration of His power and love."

The Scriptures tell us that our human struggles often provide an opportunity for our Savior to demonstrate His works to us. Without them, we would never know how much He cares. I will always remember the sacrifice Sharon and her family made that evening to be with us. I was blinded by the light. On that cold winter evening, Sharon could have easily stayed home. She was sick and in pain, yet she desperately wanted to be with us. Six days later, God called Sharon home to spend eternity with Him.

[CONTRIBUTING AUTHOR'S NOTE: *When I wrote this story, I didn't know that I also had cancer. I'm convinced that the Lord was preparing me for my own trials and tribulations.*]

THE IN SIDE by Matt Matteo

Reprinted by permission of Matt Matteo.

Darkness cannot drive out darkness; only light can do that. Hate cannot drive out hate; only love can do that.

Martin Luther King, Jr.

From Prison to Doctorate

BILL RIGGS

Billy's life was that of a typical young boy from Dallas, Texas. Early on there were years of abuse. Moving, violence, and upheaval were the norm. At age twelve, he ran away to live with his grandparents. Life settled down for a while until his grandmother died. Then at fifteen, he left home and lived on the streets of Dallas for two years. He slept behind the bushes of a community church but was never invited inside.

One day, while walking the streets of Irving, west of Dallas, he walked into a recruiter's office, ultimately enlisting in the Marines. Now a man inadequately prepared for interpersonal relationships or marriage, trouble at home made military life miserable. Billy's first marriage ended in divorce. After getting out of the service he married again, only to see it too end in divorce. This time he wound up in prison, and another single mom was on the streets.

It was during his incarceration that a prison ministry volunteer came to visit him. Tony not only taught Billy about Christ, but demonstrated the Christian way of living and the meaning of unconditional love. Billy watched Tony go through an unexpected and devastating divorce, and yet he kept coming back to visit every month.

Tony had no way of knowing the impact he was having— not so much by what he said, but how he lived. Billy learned about putting God first, others second, and himself last. Tony's consistent visits enhanced Billy's spirit and character, inspiring him to return to school. He earned his associate's degree and went on to meet a Christian woman who taught him tolerance, temperance, and acceptance. After his release, Billy went to work, obtained his electrician's license, and married the woman who loved him for who he was.

Married to the same Christian woman for seventeen years, Billy is now a master electrician. He holds a bachelor's and master's degree in psychology and a doctorate in education. An avid volunteer chaplain in the Texas Department of Criminal Justice and in the Belize Central Prison in Central America, Billy is also president of Free and Forgiven Ministries (an aftercare program that focuses on faith-based higher education) and a speaker for ministry and counseling groups throughout the United States.

Because Tony cared enough to demonstrate his faith by serving those "written off" by society, the young man from the streets of Dallas has answered God's call. *I'm that* Billy, and I continue to live my faith through service to others.

[EDITOR'S NOTE: *For more information on Free and Forgiven Ministries, contact P.O. Box 5442, Abilene, TX 79608-5442; e-mail: fandfministries@yahoo.com; website: http://prisonministry.net/frf; phone: 325-672-5802.*]

We must keep our hope, faith, and sanity by seeking ways to help others and to make a difference in our community here in prison.

Sue Ellen Allen

Silent Friends

GEORGE T. SCANLON

About seven years ago, I had the misfortune of messing with Texas and found myself incarcerated in a Houston jail. Since I was from Missouri, the judge felt I was a flight risk, so bail was denied, despite the fact that I had a clean record.

Not having done any previous jail time, I soon became disillusioned and appalled at the disgusting living conditions. I went into a deep depression that I'd never experienced before. It was during this time that I decided to write a letter to my teenage daughter. Through my own reckless stupidity, I'd missed her birthday. For me, there is no greater love than that between a father and daughter—unconditional and pure as the driven snow.

Overwhelmed by my feelings of love, sorrow, self-pity, and loneliness, I began to cry. I was so keenly tuned in to the center of my own conscience that it seemed God controlled my hand as I wrote. Suddenly I was aware of another's presence. As I looked up, I made eye contact with a young Mexican inmate. I recalled the well-known phrase, "The eyes are the windows to the soul." The inmate caught me in my moment of weakness—something that is never done in prison.

I returned his stare, challenging him to look away. He was invading my privacy, but in that instant we connected. It was as if this young man felt my pain and suffering. As I resumed writing and finished my daughter's letter, I felt better. I discovered that writing can be therapeutic.

Later on, he motioned for me to come over, sit down, and share a cup of coffee. He couldn't speak English, and I couldn't speak Spanish, so we drank our coffee in silence. I noticed his empty locker and realized he had just shared his last measure of coffee. To know he had given me all that he had in this world was humbling.

That day we became silent friends. I learned he was a long way from his home in southern Mexico, cut off from all contact with his own family, just as I was. Because neither of us had any money on our books, we didn't get commissary. We couldn't talk, but we knew each other's thoughts. The two of us were one of a kind.

Sometimes we find God in the hearts of other people before we find Him in ourselves. I left prison that fall with a new sense of purpose and determination to be the best father that God would allow me to be.

❦

In one of our experimental prison units, we had a sign posted that read, "Don't speak unless you can improve the silence." This was by far the quietest 100-man dorm in the prison. The incident rate was significantly reduced and correctional officers requested duty assignments specifically to that unit.

Dan Millstein

Lessons in Humanity

RANDY GEER

Early in my career, while processing a sixty-five-year-old Native American elder into a prison event, I noted that he was accompanied by his sons, ages three and eight. Later, I asked him what prompted him to start a family at his age. He smiled and told me, "I still have a lot to learn, and my boys are the best teachers."

Twice in my lifetime, the inmate population of the Oregon Department of Corrections (DOC) reached out to my family and me by sending flowers for a funeral. The first time was some thirty-five years ago to honor my father, who was killed in the line of duty at the Oregon State Penitentiary. The last time was recently to honor my son, Alex.

Although it may surprise some people, the compassion and respect inmates have shown my family does not surprise me, nor will it surprise many of my fellow DOC employees and inmates who are, or were, members of the Oregon State Penitentiary community.

Some of the most noble and compassionate acts I have ever witnessed were performed in prison by inmates. On the day following the sudden and senseless death of my son, I asked that several inmates across the department be informed so they wouldn't be shocked by reading the obituary, and they would know the reason why I was away from my desk and out of reach.

Our family was inundated with letters, cards, and artwork from inmates and others who heard the news through the grapevine. I placed the artwork above my desk to remind me of Alex and as a testimony to the relationships I've built with inmates through years of dialogue and cemented by hundreds of shared activities.

I continue to use the artwork to stimulate conversation about how, in my experience, corrections works best when it has a heart, a soul, and a human face. In the weeks following Alex's death, it occurred to me how often incarceration can be the last hope to intervene when a young life hangs in the balance. With the prevalence of inmates who have a diagnosed mental illness and a coexisting alcohol and drug abuse problem, many youthful offenders resemble my late son.

Alex's death by an accidental overdose caused me to reexamine and recommit to the humane principles of incarceration that the DOC has always endorsed and expected from all its employees. I promised myself to start every workday by remembering that I'm responsible for the care, safety, and growth of real people, who like my late son are desperately battling demons. These individuals are sons and daughters, brothers and sisters, as well as fathers and mothers. I can honor those universal and eternal relationships best by performing my duties with gravity, compassion, and humanity.

I learned much from my father, and I learned from my son, but I also learned and continue to learn lessons in humanity from our inmates. For their tender mercies, for their compassion, and for showing my family and the Department of Corrections the angels of their better natures, I will be forever grateful and humble.

[EDITOR'S NOTE: *This story was adapted from a letter to inmates that was published in all inmate newsletters across Oregon.*]

Let's Party

TEKLA DENNISON MILLER

Organizing the Children's Visitation Program took six months, several intrepid volunteers, ten special prisoners, and four dedicated prison employees. The primary motives of this unique visitation program for children of incarcerated mothers at Huron Valley Women's Prison were to strengthen and foster positive mother-child relations and to offer preventive intervention in the lives of children of women prisoners. Children with a parent in prison are more likely to become delinquents or criminally involved.

Each Saturday morning, children and prisoner moms participated in four hours of constructive visiting, monitored and facilitated by a volunteer Ph.D. psychologist, a volunteer social worker, one civilian prison employee, and prisoner caregivers who either had no children or whose children had been taken away from them by the courts. The visits were created to foster intimacy between mother and child and reduce the stress caused by separation. Unlike regular visits, both mother and child were allowed to move about the visiting room, and there were no uniformed officers present. Our goal was to have the program fully funded with a permanent, full-time staff person.

Children from all over the state of Michigan were transported by trained volunteer drivers in vans donated by churches. More than two hundred children were divided into four groups, one for each weekend; some hadn't seen their mothers for two or more years, and some prisoners hadn't seen their youngest child since giving birth while in prison. Many of the children arrived hungry, unwashed, and in need of tender loving care. They got it all, including a change of the court-ordered caregiver, if necessary.

Officers who came into contact with the children were chosen carefully to instill a feeling of calm and caring. On the first Saturday, two cars arrived early for the visit. The drivers decided to entertain the children, who ranged in age from four to ten years, by walking them to the ponds in front of the men's prison to see the geese nesting there. But visitors were not allowed in that area, so an officer was instructed to call the band of five children and two drivers back to the prison. I smiled as I saw the officer, all six feet five inches of him, leading a parade of children marching in a straight line, followed by the two drivers and a row of geese.

Once the children were back at the prison, they were taken through the security gates. The startled children jumped and turned around to stare at Gate 1 when it clanged shut, separating them from the familiar outside world. They were enclosed in a small room with a tall, strange man in a green and black uniform and a woman dressed the same way. Each child was pat searched, and then lined up in front of Gate 2.

A four-year-old, whimpering boy cowered in the corner farthest from where the line was forming. When it was his turn to be searched, he began to wail. Every inch of his little body shook. The officer squatted down to face the boy. "What's the problem, my man?"

The boy softened his wail, but he neither stopped crying nor answered the question. His nose began to run. The officer took some tissues from a box on the table. "Here, let's blow your nose and talk."

The frightened boy quieted as he blew his nose, and the officer wiped the boy's face. The child took several deep, shivering breaths and stopped crying. With wide eyes, he looked up at the officer.

"You know, your mama is waiting for you just on the other side of this gate. And you know what else?"

The little boy shook his head no, his body quieting.

"Well, we're going to a party, my man!"

The other children who had been watching in silence cheered. The little boy looked at them, and a large smile spread across his face.

"Can I check you out now before we go in? You know, I have to be searched, too." Then the officer motioned to the woman officer, who picked up on the message and searched the officer. After seeing this, the little boy nodded his head yes to the question. The officer pat searched him and called out, "Gate 2!"

Gate 2 slid open, and the officer turned to the other little people. "Let's party!"

The small group of children marched to the visiting room behind the officer to enjoy the first of many such Saturdays. This time they didn't notice the loud bang of the gate closing.

❦

Example is not the main thing in influencing others. It is the only thing.

Albert Schweitzer

A Steel and Concrete Christmas

ROD CARTER

It was the beginning of a three-and-a-half-year bit. I'd be spending my first Christmas in prison at age seventeen. As the judge at my trial said, "Slow down, young man!"

Prison provided me with the opportunity for introspection. Looking inward I thought, *If I'm going to get out of prison and stay out, I need to make some changes.*

Spending Christmas with five hundred guys can be brutal. Initiating festivities through seasonal flourishes, like Christmas trees, wreaths, or songs with stirring lyrics, was next to impossible.

The cell block was two tiers high. Each of the thirty cells had a bed, toilet, sink, desk, and chair, all in moldy green or queasy yellow. Our gray shirts and sand-colored pants were an ideal contrast to the navy blue staff uniforms. Over time, this lackluster sea of mind-numbing colors produced sensory deprivation.

The prison was home to cons serving out their allotted sentences. The usual tension mellowed at Christmas as an unofficial truce was struck between cons and officers. Some inmates and officers even went so far as to break the code of "No Fraternization Between Staff and Prisoners" to shake hands and converse. On any other day of the year, this would have been considered dangerous.

God showed no intention of neglecting us in this hostile environment. It was Christmas in prison—not merry, but

Christmas nonetheless. Allow me to introduce you to a few of the guys who lived on my block.

René, a muscular French Canadian, was tattooed and scarred from head to toe from prison scrapes, street fights, and involuntary arrests. Closing in on forty, he tended to leave most of the squabbles to younger cons. Once he told me, "I'm like the old baseball pitcher. I throw as hard as I ever did, but it doesn't go as fast." Like most old pitchers, warriors, and convicts, René recognized the fact that he was no longer at the top of his game. He found a pen with his name on it and began writing his memoirs; he wrote himself right out of prison. René discovered salvation through a ballpoint pen. He eventually published his autobiography and received the governor-general's award for best Canadian book of the year.

Chris, a fine-looking, athletic man in his twenties, was into sports and excelled at baseball. He combed his dark hair straight back. His case received national attention. At fourteen years old, he had been the youngest person in Canada to be sentenced to the death penalty. His sentence was later commuted to life imprisonment. The institution arranged to place him in a stable workshop and to be lodged in a cell on a range that housed younger, less volatile inmates.

A few of the older officers had taken Chris under their wing, probably because they saw something within him that resembled their own children. They unofficially adopted Chris. No doubt that humanitarian act saved him from various assaults or worse. Because these officers, like many other Canadians, were convinced of Chris's innocence, they were willing to take risks on his behalf. Several years later, Chris was released, changed his name, and relocated to a new province. He was released in the middle of the night to thwart roving news reporters. He married and lives an exemplary life.

I never saw him again, but I admire him for the Christmases he survived inside. Chris used to man the prison radio booth in the evenings. I appreciated when he'd play Bob Dylan's music; those songs kept us connected with the community to which we would one day return.

D.J. paced inside his cell. As I looked in on him that Christmas morning, he was walking in circles, stopping on occasion to gaze at his mother's photo. She had died in prison. He spent his childhood traveling through foster homes. As a troubled teenager, D.J. often spent time in jail. When I first entered prison, he took care of me, seeing that I had tobacco and papers until my first canteen arrived.

An important resource in my inner journey was our padre, a silver-haired former paratrooper. He established a special rapport with all of us, speaking each Sunday about responsibility, reconciliation, remorse, repentance, restoration, redemption, restitution, rebirth, and resurrection; they were lofty concepts, but when the padre spoke, we understood. Some of us grabbed hold of these concepts and began integrating them into our lives. Prison was a tough testing ground for practicing these principles.

The padre organized a Christmas Eve service. He recounted the Nativity with deep emotion and solemnity, and then we went back to our lonely cells. I wrote a letter home telling my parents about "the goodie bag" the prison gave us, which included butterscotch mints and a Christmas cake.

About 9:00 PM, D.J. lifted his harmonica and began playing "Silent Night." His music guided us to a foreign town in another time. The cell block teetered on the edge of something supreme.

Although we were in prison, Christmas and its sacredness were not. We wept alone, because that's done in private. That evening, no one screamed out in nightmare anguish. We slept soundly. That Christmas was simple and stunning, revolutionary and reverent.

My First Christmas in Prison

LILY SHERMAN

Assorted mouthwatering foods filled the dining room table. We had just celebrated Christmas Eve with my husband's family.

One glance at the shortbread cookies caused a flood of memories. No one could make them like my mother-in-law. Only the second Christmas since her passing, the emotions still ran deep. Crumpled wrapping paper, new gifts, and laughter filled the room. We hated to leave, but I had a sixty-mile drive ahead of me.

After getting our children settled at my father-in-law's home, I headed for my parents' house and snuggled under the comfy covers of the guest bed.

When I woke up, I didn't fully realize what day it was. My thoughts were of getting ready to leave at my dad's departure time.

I was going to prison that morning because of my father's actions over the past eighteen years. It all began at the Washington State Reformatory, serving as a Kairos volunteer. His participation grew to include many trips into prisons to help and to lead other Kairos teams. As a church member, my father helped provide a monthly worship service at the Washington Corrections Center for Women in Purdy, Washington.

This particular Sunday was his church's weekend to conduct one of these services. He invited me to come along.

Ministry team members greeted us in the parking lot. Decked out in vibrant regalia, the women reminded me of my always smartly dressed mother.

I also met two of the gentlemen. They introduced themselves to me, using different last names, claiming to be brothers. After this gullible moment, I knew this was only the beginning of the joking.

We walked into the prison, and my father informed the officer, "I made the arrangements ahead of time." Passing through a metal detector, we proceeded through a series of doors and gates, each one locking behind us. Wielding his index finger, my dad scolded, "If you don't behave, I'll leave you here." His wit made our journey seem shorter.

We arrived in the chapel and prepared for the morning service. The female inmates filed in, stopping to look us over as they passed. During the service, we sang, offered prayers, and listened attentively to the sermon. In quiet reflection during communion, it hit me. As we partook of the Body and Blood of our Lord, Jesus Christ, I thought, *I'm like these women, and they're like me. We all need the forgiveness offered by Christ's sacrifice. We all want His love.*

One woman stood out from the rest. I was struck by the sadness in her eyes, like that of a mother who has lost a child, longing to hold him in her arms. Silently, I prayed for her. *God, in Your mercy, please comfort and heal this woman. How hard it must be to spend Christmas like this.*

My dad took a few moments to share his heart with the women—it seemed as if he were the father many of them longed for. Before we left, the inmates expressed their gratitude. I noticed the woman I'd prayed for earlier. With tear-filled eyes, she uttered, "Thank you so much," as she shook the hands of each team member. When she came to me, I embraced her. In that moment, I received a Christmas gift I will treasure always.

Choosing Your Thoughts

LYNN DURHAM

Twelve women formed a circle with their chairs, filling the modest room. Mary Alice, a weekly volunteer, was the facilitator, and I was their guest. After concluding my short presentation about different ways of looking at life and why they're important, the women began to discuss some of the issues they faced.

Renee spoke first. In a raised voice, she declared, "It's just awful! My own sister can't accept the fact that I'm in prison!"

"Should she?" I asked.

"Certainly! I'm in here, aren't I? How is she going to deny it?" Renee was clear that it was a problem for her sister, Joan. The other inmates in the group agreed that Renee's sister was wrong and that she should be supportive and accepting.

I asked Renee, "Why do you think Joan should be accepting of you when you aren't willing to accept where Joan is with her feelings about *you* and your current circumstances? Do you expect her to be able to do something that you are unable or unwilling to do?"

The entire group remained quiet. No one moved. Finally, breaking the silence, Renee acknowledged, "I never thought about it in that way. I guess it must be difficult for her to deal with the fact that I'm here in prison."

Renee's anger melted into understanding. Her harsh voice and fierce appearance softened within seconds, replaced by compassion. Instead of making herself unhappy with thoughts of what her sister *should do*, Renee began to realize that she could achieve internal peace by appreciating her sister for who she truly is. Instead of attacking Joan and pushing her further away, Renee was now accepting of her sister. Today they stand an excellent chance of mending their damaged relationship.

We talked about how holding one thought could cause them pain and how looking at circumstances in a new way could lead to peace.

Mary Alice told me later that when the group met the following week, they were still excited about the concept they had learned the week before. They continued to discuss the different ways one can look at life—how negative, judgmental thoughts lead to pain and how positive, compassionate thoughts lead to inner and outer peace.

They were impressed by their power to control their feelings, simply by choosing their own thoughts.

"NO CHERYL, THIS CELL DOESN'T MAKE YOU LOOK FAT!"

Reprinted by permission of Christian Snyder.

Practice What You Preach

DOUGLAS BURGESS

Beginning my sentence in a high-security institution twenty-three years ago, I met the stereotypical convicts, but I also met many whose incarceration had changed them for the better. They were the generous, compassionate ones who were at peace in an environment that was anything but peaceful. It took me twenty years to realize that the peace surrounding some inmates and not others was due to their relationship with Christ Jesus.

Not so long ago, the violent world in which I must live nearly ran into me as I returned to my cell from work. As two guys stormed into the hallway, they began cursing one another intently—oblivious to the fact that they almost knocked me down. As they passed out of the officer's sight, their threats and profanity accelerated to the point where they squared off, readying themselves for a fight or worse. As I was on good terms with both, I didn't want to see either get hurt or into trouble, so I took a deep breath and stepped between them.

Stepping between two guys who want to fight wasn't the smartest thing I've done in a while, especially as I took note of just how big they were while I tried to talk them out of swinging or grabbing a weapon.

Omar, a thick-chested weight lifter, was matched by Will, who at six feet three inches was equally powerful enough to squish me like a bug if things got out of hand. Holding them apart was too much for me, so I recited my favorite beatitude as a means of prayer: "Blessed are the peacemakers, for they will be called sons of God." Will's anger evaporated, and he let me gently push him away from Omar, who seemed only too happy to use this opportunity to stomp off to his cell while spitefully hurling a few colorful curses over his shoulder.

Will caught up with me later that day and started to apologize, "I'm afraid I've failed as a Christian."

Raising my hand high enough to reach his shoulder, I interrupted. "You owe me no apology, Will. This is what Christ expects of His flock." Then I asked, "Would you like to pray to the Lord for His forgiveness and His strength to apologize to the men who witnessed you acting in other than a Christlike manner?"

Will nodded his agreement. So we did, and then he did, going man to man, ensuring none were left out. Now my friend is attending church with me and putting into practice the peace that Christ preached.

One of the factors that gives me peace and allows me to cope with prison is that I know touching someone's life in prison has equal, if not more, impact than touching someone's life in society.

John Schmidt

My Former Self

TROY EVANS

As I put the key into the lock of my front door and swung it open, I discovered that the contents of my hallway closet were spread along the carpet. Going from room to room, I discovered that the whole house was in disarray. Every drawer had been pulled out and overturned. Our house was a complete mess.

My wife and I were burglarized that day. We lost everything we owned of value: TV, VCR, computer, stereo, and jewelry that had been handed down to my wife for generations. Some things could never be replaced. Was I mad? Did I want to get my hands on the people who had done this to me? You better believe I did.

Several days later as I was sitting in my office filling out the insurance forms, I wondered, *Why did this happen to me?*

Gradually it became clear. I had never been on that end of things. I had always been the thief—the taker. I never knew what it felt like to be the victim, to be taken from, to feel vulnerable.

Then it came to me. *Maybe I need to feel that. Maybe this was the final nail in the coffin of the old Troy Evans being buried and put away forever without the possibility of him ever returning to his former self.*

Beyond the Walls

PATRICIA H. MARTIN

Teaching English 101: Craft of Composition at a women's correctional facility is a joy. The classroom has no officers or shackles; decorum depends on a group of respectful women eagerly pursuing their education. I enjoy the subject matter, the challenge, and my students.

Rowena is articulate. Her interests span the gamut from physical fitness to creation mythology. Free time finds her either in the gym or the library. She is an intellectual. For one assignment she wrote about the vibration of air. Last month she was released. I wish her well.

Jolene is a lifer. In her words, "I'm a *word* not a number." A woman whose sentence is a *number* is eligible for parole sooner than a woman who is a *word*. Another student was upset at being denied parole. Jolene reasoned with her like a counselor. Her fellow students agree she always has something positive to say. Halfway through the course, she received a *ticket* for a clothing rule infraction and was put in lockup. She failed the course.

A woman of few words, Tonia is also a lifer. In the first class her only words were, "Get me out of here." Tonia believes people can learn from their mistakes and change their lives. She expressed dismay that some criminals receive a life sentence without the possibility of parole. When I read that, I had the feeling her essay was autobiographical. I hope I'm wrong.

At forty-seven, Violet is the oldest and the best writer of the group. Whether writing a subjective description, a narrative, or a persuasive piece, her logical mind is expressed in a rich vocabulary. Her inspired writing requires little revision. Violet's job is keeping the infirmary clean. Two teenagers are currently on suicide watch in the infirmary. Violet visits them whenever she can to console them. This summer Violet expects to be a free woman. I tell her, "Keep writing." She is gifted and deserves to see her work published.

The second best writer, Starlet, struggles with her class work and uses her dictionary often when reading and writing. She reads aloud nervously but writes well. Starlet says, "I have to read sentences a couple of times to understand them." When I examine her papers, it's hard to believe she has difficulty. I know it's her work because her writing is consistent, whether it's done in her cell or in class. Starlet's classmates envy her. She has the best-paying job—typing prison data into a computer.

Tobie, an energetic math whiz, is ready for release soon. She hopes to move to Atlanta, attend college, and major in math. Grateful for her incarceration, she admitted, "If I hadn't come to prison, my drug habit would have killed me." She passed her GED, attended parenting classes, and learned electrical and plumbing skills. "Once I quit drugs, I realized I was intelligent," she said.

It was a blessing to be part of such a positive educational program. These college courses take the students beyond the walls, bring them some sense of normalcy, and give substance to their dreams.

Show Compassion, Lend a Hand, Make a Difference

TOM LAGANA AND LAURA LAGANA

4.1 What is your definition and understanding of the word "compassion"?

4.2 What recent examples of compassion have you noticed, either demonstrated by you or someone else?

4.3 What are you already doing to help others?

4.4 What more can you do to help others?

4.5 How does helping someone else make you feel?

4.6 Thinking about the crimes you have committed, answer the following:
How do you think your victims felt?
How do you think they feel now?
How would you feel if someone did this to you?

FIVE

Awakening
the Spirit

My cellmate and I pray together daily, and our
prayers are often answered in incredible ways.
Prayer shows us that God is working behind the
scenes where we can't go. Some things that
happen have no other explanation. We can call it
luck or coincidence, but I choose to call it faith.
It's like the air we breathe or the love we feel.
We can't see it, but we know it's there. It's the
same thing with God. We can't see Him, but we
know He's there.

SUE ELLEN ALLEN

Little Did I Know

KEN FOX

For no apparent reason I hated people. I used to be the most angry, bitter, and judgmental person on the planet. I mistreated the few who still loved me despite my atrocious behavior, including the woman who I now realize is a gift from God. She has to be an angel. How else could she have loved me and stood by me through fifteen years of this stuff?

About two and a half years ago, I transferred to a facility nearly four hours away from home. Being cut off from friends and family not only fueled my anger, it also gave me a reason to distrust the supposedly merciful and loving God my fiancée loved so dearly.

Once I arrived at the prison, I lashed out at this wonderful woman. "What do you think about *your* God now?" I bellowed. A cheap shot I know, but I didn't care.

Not long after that I received a letter from my cousin. I hadn't heard from her in five years. It was at her request and the encouragement of my fiancée that I looked into Keryx. This program, a Christian weekend for inmates, is similar to Kairos. I sought out two Christian guys in my housing unit and asked if they knew anything about the program. They were happy to talk with me, but without my knowledge they approached the chaplain about getting me into the upcoming Keryx weekend.

Still carrying a large chip on my shoulder and anger in my heart, I reluctantly agreed to attend but not before delivering a

firm warning. My fists waving in the air, I shrieked, "If anyone tries to hug me, I swear I'll swing first and ask questions
later!" I was convinced the weekend would have no effect on
me.

For the first day of the weekend, I managed to keep my distance. I was certain that I'd won and that God had nothing to
offer me. I aimed to prove it, but on the third day something
happened. All the walls I'd built up around myself—my false
securities and all that I'd come to count on to keep myself safe
and distant—began to collapse.

Earlier that day one of the volunteers told me the Holy
Spirit had something in store for me. I smiled and shrugged it
off for as long as I could. After that, we were asked to close
our eyes and bow our heads. I complied and waited for further
instructions.

As I sat there, the room suddenly filled with unfamiliar
voices. Songs of praise ushered in the overwhelming presence
of God. My heart began to swell with emotion. I'd never felt
such an intense love.

At that moment, the destructive and negative feelings that
I'd built up inside poured forth in nonstop tears. I had no control over my thoughts, my feelings, or my body. The Holy
Spirit had arrived, and without a doubt, He had kicked my
butt!

For the remainder of that weekend, I didn't allow anyone to
pass without giving them a hug. My heart of stone had crumbled. My walls had tumbled down. The light of the Lord illu-
minated my heart where darkness once ruled.

Yes, God came looking for me that day. Since getting a hold
on me, He refuses to let go. I still have my rough days. The trials and temptations are still there, but the love of God sees me
through, because I know brighter days are ahead.

Now, to answer the question I asked my fiancée two and a
half years ago, "What do I think of *her* God now?" I think *our*

God is an awesome God, and I thank Him for loving a wretch like me.

[EDITOR'S NOTE: *Keryx is a Greek word meaning "herald." Similar to Kairos, Keryx is an interdenominational ministry, a volunteer-based, three-day weekend based on Cursillo. For information on Keryx Michigan Prison Ministry, visit the websites: www.chippewakeryx.org or www.cursillos.ca/en/ expansion/groupes/keryx.htm. Outside of Michigan, for information on Kairos Prison Ministry International, visit the website at www.kairosprisonministry.org; write to 6903 University Blvd., Winter Park, FL 32792; or phone: 407-629-4948.*]

There are many positive things in every day if a person is willing to let go of the negative and embrace the positive. The bottom line is that the decisions I made in the past are what have me sitting in prison today, and I accept full responsibility for this. I know that things happen for a reason and ultimately all of the obstacles that I've faced in my life have made me a stronger, more determined person today. I am fortunate in so many ways, and I have a real sense of gratitude for the blessings that God has filled my life with. It would be selfish of me to waste my energy dwelling on the negative.

Dave LeFave

Seeking Peace

KENNETH E. HARTMAN

It is said that within the most powerful storm dwells an eye of tranquillity, a place of solace. Within the tempest of life, everyone needs to find his own place of refuge. For those of us who reside in prison, the need to find such a place is even more imperative.

From time immemorial, man has sought contact with the transcendent. The tales of these quests reverberate through the ages: Buddha sitting under a tree for weeks in silent contemplation of what is and what is not; Moses climbing the mountain to come face to face with the fiery image of his God.

Native Americans set off on vision quests into a wilderness of primeval forests. Many of these journeys lasted weeks, months, or even longer. The traveler was celebrated upon his return while his compatriots waited for the wisdom gleaned by the ordeal. And what was Jesus's suffering and death on the cross if not a trek?

The common denominator of these odysseys is the element of suffering and hardship. In the long years of my sojourn through the prison system, removed from my family and loved ones, scorned by strangers, and demonized by the media, I have come to find something extraordinary. The handiwork of God is to be found here, if one cares to look.

I look. In the early mornings a prison is rife with expectancy, coiled noise, and chaos, as we wait to break out of our little hovels. I lay awake in my bed and open myself to the energy flowing through the building. I still the voice inside that cries out for attention, and sometimes I hear the music, the gentle lapping of waves against the beach of time.

True quiet is the key to peace. Everyone needs to set aside a regular period of time every day; a time to be quiet and resist the endless fidget that defines our culture. Tribesmen in the Amazon rain forest, on first encountering Western man, were astounded at the pace of our lives and our desire to accumulate things. As if these totems could somehow save us from the fate of all living things—the end of our earthly existence.

Once I was told I would soon die from a terminal disease. Unlike those in the "free world," I was not given drugs to numb me out, nor was I able to use the distractions of materialism to ward off my sadness. Isolated, locked away in a four-by-ten-foot cell while I prepared to die in the span of several months, I found my true self.

I struggled and ultimately fell to the floor exhausted, before I gave in to the stillness. In that place of utter blackness I stood in front of a chasm, deep and immense. It terrified me. Then, without warning, I fell into a virtual abyss, tumbling into nothingness.

During my experience, the nothingness became warm and inviting, like sweet, thick, nourishing honey. The stillness has never frightened me again. Tranquillity is a coat to be worn in tough times—a shelter from the wind. One must step off into the dark, alone, away from the lights and intrusions of the modern world. It is in the terror of the fall that one finds the next key to peace.

Long ago, when I was a young man filled with pain and rage, I struck out at the world. I worked hard to remove myself from humanity. Some would say I became a monster. Others might say I am still a monster. I suspect that I felt the ringing wail of what was missing in my life more keenly than most. The empty confusion, the incomprehensible, filled me with fear.

I now realize that I have nothing to fear and nothing to desire. I am okay. That is the final key to peace. In my heart of hearts, I know the storm of my life is but a puff of air in the great whirlwind of the cosmos.

I encourage you to seek your peace. Open your heart to the wind rushing in and out of your lungs, the rhythm of life. I breathe the same air that everyone else does, the air that every newborn cries out to taste. Just be still and listen. Can you hear it?

I feel a degree of wisdom in myself from the adversity of prison that otherwise never would have been there. Having all of my possessions, titles, and connections removed, I'm left with only myself and the ability to reflect on who I am and who I should be. I'm more patient and my values are no longer superficial.

Matt Matteo

Journey of Faith

MELISSA L. CRAFT

My journey with God began as a sophomore in high school at a summer church camp. My faith journey, however, began when I found myself unmarried and pregnant. My first reaction was to rely on the coping skills I'd acquired in my earlier years. I began to separate myself emotionally and spiritually from what was going on, and more important, to the one who could help me the most—God.

I felt so ashamed that I couldn't turn to Him. I began to work on "fixing the problem." I promptly made the call and scheduled the appointment. I remember that Saturday morning like it was yesterday. God has an unusual way of giving us wake-up calls when we need them most. Before we left for the appointment, I had my first sign. This was God's way of shouting, "Hey, you! Yes, *you*, the pregnant one. Wake up!"

We continued on to our destination. I was still convinced that this "problem" needed to be corrected that day; God, however, had a different outcome for me. We must have driven past the clinic twenty times, each time with my heart growing heavier. I knew I couldn't do this. This "problem," as I called it to help me cope, was a beautiful living baby, formed in God's image, growing inside me.

Needless to say, I didn't go through with *my* way of fixing the "problem." I totally gave it over to God. I remember saying, "God, please use me and this experience to grow your

Kingdom. I know there's a reason and purpose for this. Please reveal it to me in Your time."

That was one of the hardest phases of my life. I was blessed to have a loving family and friends to help me through it, but most of all, I knew God was with me. Throughout my pregnancy, God kept revealing little glimpses of what He might have in mind. I kept running into young, unmarried, pregnant girls. After giving birth to my beautiful boy, God finally revealed His will for me.

One of the recurring themes throughout my pregnancy was the loneliness and my need to share my experiences with others who would understand. With help and support from loved ones, churches, and God, I started a support group. For almost five years, we helped girls and women of different races and ages. During that time, God also directed my career path. Leading the group helped me realize that I needed to return to school. After turning thirty, I earned my master's in social work.

As I sit here and look at Jonathan's picture, I feel sad. It's difficult for me to believe that my beautiful child began to use drugs in the eighth grade. That was the beginning of years of agony and pain, riddled with bitterness and anger. In the ninth grade, Jonathan began getting into trouble—not at school but with the law. From then until he turned eighteen, he went to the Department of Juvenile Justice Evaluation Center twice and once to their wilderness camp for four months. That was just the beginning of countless sleepless nights and days where I asked myself, *Where did I go wrong?*

I tried everything to get him help. I must have worn a hole in the carpet from pacing and praying. I didn't know what to do. I asked God to help. He helped release me from my guilt. God helped me to realize that Jonathan was making his own choices, ones over which I had no control. While this provided temporary relief, nothing prepared me for the shock of seeing my boy being handcuffed, shackled, and led off to a place where I couldn't be with him. No parent should ever have to witness something like this. I will remember that day for the rest of my life. Looking back, I know this was only the tip of the iceberg. God was preparing me for the worst.

When he was eighteen, Jonathan was arrested two more times. On one of these charges, he was awaiting a court date, and on the other he was required to serve two months in county jail. He distanced himself from his family, refusing to answer his cell phone. We constantly wondered where he was and if he was safe.

During this time, my faith journey grew even more challenging. I prayed for my child to be saved. I asked God to protect him and bring him home. I remember being so desperate that I asked God to sacrifice my life, if that is what it would take, so that my son would come to know Him and walk in His ways. Ever since that Saturday morning so many years ago, I have always known God has a purpose for Jonathan. I wanted and needed him to know this.

I remember the last time I saw Jonathan on the outside. It was late February. As I drove through my neighborhood and turned the corner, I spotted him, in a ragged T-shirt and jeans, sitting on the water drain along the curb. I tried to convince him to come home with me, but he didn't utter a word. He even refused to acknowledge my presence. I drove away in tears, begging God to watch over him.

Nowadays, my Saturday mornings consist of rising at 6:00 AM to prepare for the allotted four-hour visit with my son. I've become accustomed to this routine over the last year; it's one I'm resigned to keep for the next seven.

Although it might sound sad, I know all of this was God's answer to my prayers. I was convinced that if Jonathan stayed on the path he was on, he was either going to die, be killed, or be responsible for someone's death before he turned nineteen.

As when I discovered I was pregnant, I asked God to reveal to me His purpose and will. But I hadn't planned on or prepared myself for God's answer.

Last year, I sent Jonathan a Bible. On my first visit after he had received it, he was quoting Scripture. He told me all about his love for the Word. I noticed the sparkle and excitement in his eyes when he talked about God. He seemed to know that God has a plan for him, too.

Today Jonathan is doing well. He has been moved to a different facility. When I shared with him my anxiety about his pending move, he said, "Mom, this is the journey that God has for me now."

For I know the plans I have for you," declares the Lord, "plans to prosper you and not to harm you, plans to give you hope and a future."

Jeremiah 29:11

Crisis of Faith

ROLAND PECK

S ervices that day were ordinary; that is, if you consider wor-
shipping God in a "church" that consists of a cyclone-fenced
yard topped with loops of razor wire and an altar that serves as
a garbage can the other six days of the week to be ordinary.

Placing my communion box on the overturned can, I noticed
the amazing view from the yard. I doubt that many maximum
security prisons feature magnificent vistas that rival those seen
from San Quentin. From the vantage point of the exercise
yards, the upper reaches of San Francisco Bay are visible,
backgrounded by the majesty of Mount Tamalpais. The tranquillity of the region contradicts the realities of prison life.

As I surveyed the area, my gaze was once again captured by
the anguished expression on the face of a lone man I had noticed
a few minutes earlier, leaning against the fence. He seemed
despondent and alienated, preferring to stand on the fringes of
the immediate "church" area. I wasn't surprised when he turned
down my invitation to join the service. I was surprised, though,
when he unexpectedly asked, "May I speak with you privately
before you leave the yard, sir?" Naturally, I agreed.

After the service, my new friend walked cautiously toward
me. I asked him if he wanted to share his burden with me.
Hesitating at first, he finally broke the silence. "I was a gang-
banger on the outside. I just got orders from the highest-
ranking member of my gang, here on the inside, that they want
me to kill a fellow prisoner." He explained that the "code"

required he accept the vendetta and succeed with the execution or else forfeit his own life.

His conscience wouldn't allow him to carry out such an act, but he didn't want to die either. Looking me in the eyes, he asked, "What do you think I should do?"

I've always considered myself to be a person of strong moral fiber with a solid grasp of Christian principles, but when confronted with this life-and-death situation, all I could muster was a handful of religious platitudes and Sunday school answers.

After I went home that day and for weeks afterward, I beat myself up for not saying all the sage things I could have said. If only I had thought of them at the time. As I Monday-morning-quarterbacked my actions, I was brought back to one of my shortcomings—underestimating God's power. I realized I wasn't the center of this drama—God was.

Two weeks later, I was reminded of His great power when I encountered my friend once again, only this time he was smiling. Instead of sitting off against the fence, he willingly participated in the church service. I couldn't wait to talk with him after the service to learn what he had decided to do.

He smiled, held his head high, and said, "Mr. Peck, I've decided to be on God's side."

That was the "right" answer, the one you might expect in the movies. Only this wasn't the movies. I was compelled against my calling to ask if he was absolutely sure of his decision, knowing that his failure to kill another person could result in great personal harm or even death. Part of me was wondering, *How can I live with myself knowing that my advice might be the catalyst that gets another man killed?*

When my gutsy friend restated, "I want to be on God's side," I realized that it was *my* faith that was lacking. The courage this man displayed for disobeying an order handed down by the gang was indeed humbling. This man was willing to stand up for his beliefs, even if it meant putting his own life on the line. This devout inmate had no doubts or limits on *his* faith in the power and ability of God.

I never learned what actually transpired, but I did see my friend once again after that. He simply told me, "My decision was the right one." He reassured me that he was still on God's side, and he wanted to stay that way.

As we talked, the topic of faith came up. He expressed concern that perhaps his faith wasn't as strong as it should be. Thinking of the heroic decision he had made, I quoted Matthew 17, "the mustard seed story," and assured him that his recent deeds were strong enough to "move mountains."

My new friend came to me for help with his faith, but he taught me about living it.

THE IN SIDE by Matt Matteo

Reprinted by permission of Matt Matteo.

God's Loving Hands

KYLE "QUILLY" QUILAUSING

I can't wait until my freedom can shine,
This day will come in a matter of time.
Seconds tick as minutes pass,
I will erase memories of my haunting past.

Hours that drag slowly turn into days,
But I am bettering myself in many ways.
Months go by that add up to years,
Time has dried up all of my tears.

I ask the Lord to cleanse my heart,
To prepare my life for a brand-new start.
I'm determined to succeed, I have no doubts,
Because my Heavenly Father will help me out.

I will make wise choices to achieve my goals,
I will try my best with my heart and soul.
If my heart could speak, it would likely say,
"I will never fail you nor go astray."

My life will be happy, plain, and quite simple,
Because I was blessed when I needed a miracle.
God's promises will prevail and His love will prosper,
God is my savior and there will be no other.

Day by day, blessings unfold,
"Stay faithful to God," is what I was told.
I know in my heart what I must do,
To have eternal life I must follow His rules.

I pray the Lord my soul to take,
And please forgive all my mistakes.
I was once weak, but now I stand
Since I was touched by God's loving hands.

❧ ❧

I know that I can't change the past and that the future is in God's hands. This gives me a genuine sense of peace and makes my incarceration more tolerable.

Dave LeFave

A Place Closer to God

GRACE CLARK

On the north side of the prison property, a potholed and muddy dirt road runs parallel to the wire fence of the compound and beyond, into a wooded area. I drive in, perhaps a quarter of a mile off the paved highway, to a lodge-style wooden building. A porch with picnic tables and rocking chairs lines the length of both sides of the structure. A large banquet room and several small private dining rooms are in the middle. The commercial-style kitchen is a huge room with stoves, sinks, work tables, huge pots and pans, pastry boards, and a well-stocked pantry.

A few steps from the kitchen door is a towering barbecue fireplace. Stacks of split wood stand an arm's-length from the pit. Screened racks await chicken halves that will be arranged on top of them for tonight's barbecue dinner. Johnny is the cook. This is his kitchen. Johnny is an inmate, a trustee in a white uniform. He has a reputation for having the best chicken barbecue in northeast Florida. A popular spot for lunch meetings, officers must call ahead for reservations at Johnny's.

Today at Johnny's, the team is preparing meals for the Kairos weekend. When Kairos is held in a male prison, female cooking teams serve only from outside the prison confines. I am one of these women.

A team of forty men from surrounding cities have come to spend four days on this weekend, bringing God's love and fellowship to forty-two inmates in this maximum security prison.

As we unload the cars and truck, moving boxes of food into the kitchen, I hear sharp noises. The lodge is on the rifle range. Target practice is going on at four different stations. We continue as if they were not there, feeling honored to be serving God and mankind in this special way: making sandwiches, cutting fruit, and arranging everything artistically. Platters heaping with sandwiches and fresh fruit, covered with plastic wrap, are ready for the 11:00 AM Kairos lunch break.

We all pitch in and load the food into the van for its journey to the prison gates. Holding hands, we encircle the food and bless it. Hundreds of homemade cookies are already in the prison awaiting distribution by the bagful. As the truck drives off, we take a few minutes to relax until it's time to begin preparing for the supper meal.

Some wild blackberry bushes surrounding the small mound behind Johnny's Kitchen catch my eye. I go blackberry picking, popping each into my mouth as I climb the mound. Reaching the top, I clean off a spot to sit.

What a view. In the distance across an open field, I can see the prison's west fence and guard tower. The education building and top of the chapel roof are dwarfed by the distance, but I can still identify them. In the southwest corner sits the residential complex. I know my husband is serving as a clergyman on the Kairos team inside those buildings. I also know our son is serving as a musician—my husband wearing his clerical collar garb, our son dressed in his state-issued blues.

The mound descends a gradual slope to a dry drainage ditch. The graveyard for men who have died with no one to claim their bodies lies just on the other side of the ditch. Simple crosses mark each grave. The crosses bear no names, only a number—isolation and anonymity. They say that when a man dies and they are ready to bury him in this potters' field, the chaplain conducts a service with the inmates. The close friends of the deceased are in attendance. I understand that the chaplain recently had the policy changed so that the crosses now bear the inmates' names.

The spot on top of this mound is a sacred place for me. I can see how God has worked in my life, bringing our family to a place where we can serve God in a special way. I pray for the prison compound. I pray for the Kairos program. I pray for the officers who have to keep up their skills to do their job well. I pray for Johnny, who has earned the right to be a trustee and have a positive relationship with his officers. I pray for the families who were unaware of, or chose to ignore, the death of their family member. I thank God for placing the blackberries here to grow in the midst of that which symbolizes evil.

As we prepare the supper, I take a few minutes every now and then to retreat to my sacred place outside. God is here. We talk together. At supper time, I watch as kettles of chili, boxes of French bread, salad, and apple pie are loaded into the truck and transported to the Kairos site. My work is finished.

Tiny rays of sunshine filter through the leaves, which stir slightly in a gentle whisper of a breeze. A squirrel scampers across a grave, picks up a nut, and carries it away. The setting sun shines its beams on the wire fence, making the razors shimmer. Target practice ends with one last gunshot. There I sit, on the miniature mountain behind Johnny's Kitchen, my sacred place for contemplation, where I am closer to God.

[EDITOR'S NOTE: *For information on Kairos Prison Ministry International, visit the website at www.kairo sprisonministry.org; write to 6903 University Blvd., Winter Park, FL 32792; or phone 407-629-4948.*]

Love Conquers All

DICK WITHEROW

The new warden ordered the chaplain to add a Muslim to her staff of inmate orderlies. She did as she was told, and then sparks began to fly.

As I walked into the chapel, I came upon several inmates in a confrontational attitude. Barry, the newest member of the chaplain orderly staff, was under attack. He was the first Muslim to be chosen to join the staff, along with six Christian orderlies. The Christians were quoting Scripture in an effort to convince Barry to abandon his Muslim beliefs and embrace Christianity. Their efforts were not getting the desired results, as Barry was showing his displeasure with what was happening. Normally Barry was a gentle giant. He enjoyed being around people and had a winning smile.

After Barry left the chapel, I talked to the other orderlies. "You won't be able to convert Barry by arguing with him. Just try to accept him as he is, and love on him." I had no problem setting an example in this respect since Barry was such a lovable guy. I made it a point, as I came to the prison to facilitate the Alcoholics Victorious Group each week, to engage Barry in conversation. Although he seemed to enjoy my company, he always walked out when our meeting started.

Several weeks after our initial meeting, I asked him, "Why don't you hang around a while, at least until I've shared a testimony of what God has done to save several members of my immediate family." He honored my request and then left immediately afterward.

Three weeks later, I was greeted by an obviously enthusiastic Barry. "Dick, guess what? I'm a believer. I've come to know that Jesus is the Messiah, and I've made Him my Lord." Barry went on to explain his concern over how he was going to tell his mother. You see, he had been raised a Shiite Muslim.

Then his face lit up with a big grin as he said, "I received a letter from my mother this morning. She started out by telling me how worried she was. She wondered how I would accept the fact that she became a Christian."

I crossed my arms and beamed. "You don't say."

❧

There are many names for God. There are many directions to Him. God has created a beautiful bouquet of faiths. Let our Christianity be enhanced through interfaith exchange, remembering there is no handle on the cross.

Rod Carter

Yuletide Santa

KARL B. STRUNK

A wakened by a clatter, I moan and rub my eyes. It's nearly dawn on Christmas. The noise that shatters the silence is not that of St. Nicholas and eight tiny reindeer stirring atop the roof. It's my cellmate tossing about and snoring on the bunk above. On any other morning, I would have gently interrupted his sleep so I could selfishly return to that dream-filled state known as the Land of Nod. But there is no sense in attempting to claim an extra forty winks. I'm too excited.

Rolling out of bed, I proceed to freshen up for the day's adventures. Tiptoeing so as to not disturb my cellmates, I don a navy blue and green sweatshirt my mother gave me many holiday seasons ago. Closing my eyes, it feels as if my mother's arms are gently hugging me.

As the morning unfolds, I prepare for my role as Secret Santa. You see, in the week prior, I solicited contributions from fellow prison inmates on behalf of Jason, an older man down on his luck and without any financial means.

Jason is a cantankerous individual without many friends. It's not that people dislike him, but at eighty-two, he's slow at getting around and seldom ventures beyond his cell. Occasionally he journeys outdoors and putters about, but the effort it requires tires him out for the remainder of the day.

In fact, Jason conforms to our image of Santa, a gentle, squat man with chubby cheeks. Did I mention his fluffy white beard? It's real, though I haven't the audacity to tug on it.

Sadly, the "powers that be" found it necessary to fit Jason with modern eyeglasses, corrupting his jolly semblance. But what if you slid a pair of reading spectacles to the tip of his nose?

Leaving his cell for lunch, Jason smiles and extends a greeting when passing by. He seems stunned that I'm not responsive, causing me to feel shallow. This behavior on my part is an attempt at maintaining anonymity. As Jason moves out of sight, access to his cell is arranged so a bounty of unexpected treasures, about forty pounds of foodstuffs and toiletries, can be secretly displayed on top of his bed.

While in Jason's quarters, I take stock of the lack of possessions. Jason has nothing to claim as his own, not even a picture of family or friends or a measly secondhand magazine. Then my unsuspecting eyes behold one exception resting on his shelf—a threadbare Bible.

The day eventually gives way to evening, and Jason knocks at my door. Lower lip quivering, eyes swollen and red, he inquires about the alms that appeared. His voice, not quite breaking but lacking firmness, touches me. I try but fail at maintaining an impassive face. The noticeable emotions expressed in his appearance alone would cause any person to melt, but the cracking in his voice makes me smile so grandly that tears well up. I break into laughter, not at Jason, but at myself for folding so easily.

What I find most amazing is that a community of people who enjoy few belongings and yearn for so much, who are stereotyped as heartless, hardened criminals for an immoral mistake in their past, possess the inherent compassion to freely give that which they otherwise hunger for themselves—willing to go without so that another inmate they may scarcely know could experience a memorable holiday.

"NO, YOU DON'T SNORE — I'M MAKING IT UP!"

Reprinted by permission of Christian Snyder.

Have patience with all things, but chiefly have patience with yourself. Do not lose courage in considering your own imperfections, but instantly set about remedying them—every day begin the task anew.

St. Francis de Sales

The Artist

CARLA WILSON

One afternoon during my regular shift, Dave arrived at the block. Several inmates met me at the door, eager to inform me there was "an artist" in the house. Anytime an inmate who has a teachable skill or a special talent arrives, we encourage him to pass that gift on to the others. The sharing of expertise not only passes time, it also helps create an element of cohesiveness on our block, allowing our unit to function as a community.

In many ways, our unit works like a treatment center. The inmates are given strategies to help them begin looking at "self"—the foundation of all treatment models. For those who live on the inside, these walls can readily trigger a reminder of pain and turmoil. It's next to impossible for an inmate to arise each morning and not be reminded of the life from which he is now separated.

Within this culture a certain reality exists that is like no other—a reality that is almost never safe to disclose. A person must make a conscious decision to not take on the characteristics of this unpleasant environment.

Dave told me his career ended at the factory after putting in more than twenty-six years. Other personal issues, particularly the loss of his wife and family, complicated his outlook on life. He confided, "I went on a self-destructive rampage. I was out of control. I hated my life, but I didn't know how to stop . . . until I was arrested. It sounds crazy but

. . . I'm actually relieved I'm in here." Dave's way of thinking is one shared by many others. It often takes coming to jail to stop the madness and insanity.

When Dave entered the unit, he noticed an inmate seated at a table, drawing a picture. Within minutes Dave was drawing too. During the years he worked at the factory, much of his free time was spent sketching coworkers and friends. He often heard comments about the special "gift" he possessed. It was something he took for granted.

Dave sat down and began sharing his skills with other artists in the room. Before long, some observant inmates asked if he would sketch them, and a line began to form. As I watched his drawings take shape, Dave spoke freely, "I feel exhilarated knowing I'm bringing joy to the spirits of people I sketch." Dave admitted to feeling a connection that was beyond words. "It's better than getting high the way I used to. Years ago, while I was in jail, I used to draw strictly for commissary items. It was a good way to keep from going hungry, but this time is different. It's as if God is telling me something. Of course, he has my attention now. I'm in here."

While his creation took shape, Dave mentioned that a few years before, the chaplain at a treatment center asked, "What do you do when you want to be close to God?"

Dave replied, "I draw!" For the first time in years, Dave was able to reconnect with what drives him spiritually.

❦

A musician must make music, an artist must paint, a poet must write, if he is to be ultimately at peace with himself.

Abraham Maslow

The Lady and the Bird

DERRICK K. OSORIO

Several months ago, I lost someone special. I knew it was coming. She told me that although I had many wonderful qualities, patience and compassion were not among them. She was right.

God knew my pain and blessed me with a compassionate woman who came into my life at a crucial point. In her letters, Diana Marie shared her love for birds.

After losing her mother, she needed a friend. We grew to be pen pals and made arrangements to meet during the Christmas holidays. Sadly, it never happened because of her work schedule.

Wanting to experience the joys of life that enflamed her passions, I began to peer out my window in search of birds. God sent a beautiful pigeon to deliver His message. Mostly black, she was sprinkled with gray patches and white spots. I think I was more afraid of her than she was of me.

Then I noticed she had an injured leg. My heart cried out to her as she hobbled around. I crumbled cheese crackers and scattered them on the sill. She gobbled them up. As I watched her, my mind drifted. I wondered, *Lord, what are You trying to tell me?*

Eventually more feathered friends arrived and my windowsill was full of birds. I named the fluffy black one D.M. after my bird-loving friend, Diana Marie. "Jesus loves you," I said. D.M. looked up at me as though she understood.

My heart ached. In my sorrow, I looked at D.M. and wondered what I could do to help. She seemed to be in pain as she limped across the sill. I felt powerless.

As the days passed, she seemed to improve. She would sing to me as she announced her arrival and her ravenous appetite. I became familiar with her feeding times and looked forward to her visits.

I was amazed at the wonder of God's feathered aviators. Each day brought more varieties. It was as if they had broadcast to the other birds, "Over here! The softy in cell 225 is putting out a spread!" They had grown accustomed to their buffet. I even added pretzels and other tidbits to the menu.

I also learned how territorial these birds can be. They squabble over their food and have their feeding zones all picked out. Before indulging in her smorgasbord, D.M. perched on my sill and looked around for competition.

Birds are a lot like humans. We get attached to someone we love to the point that we don't want to let them go. We feel a sense of ownership and put our claim on the lives of those we care about—something I've done to others and others have done to me.

I grew fond of D.M. One afternoon she failed to return. For weeks I waited, but no D.M. I missed her. She helped me realize that if you love someone, you need to let them go. You must give them the freedom to search out their own happiness. If they are meant to be in your life, they will return.

About this same time, Diana Marie stopped writing to me. Although we never met in person, she left me with spiritual insight into God's marvelous creation and the precious gifts He has given to us.

❦

In prison we have a chance to learn all the things we thought we already knew. The most painful things that have happened in my life, I have learned the most from.
                                        Kathy Zimmerman

I Finally Saw the Light

JIMMY HUFF

My mother was a God-fearing woman, but my alcoholic father drank up our family's grocery money. Dad was a sick person who couldn't help himself. He used to beat us when he got drunk. Along with my five brothers and five sisters, I lived in constant terror. I grew up hating my childhood.

In addition to her own brood, my mother raised five grandchildren. We moved around a lot, never staying in one place for more than a year or two. Dad tried his hand at farming, but we kids did all the work, which was why we were always late for school.

The only one in my family to earn a high school diploma, I graduated from Colorado High in 1963. I joined the navy right away, and they sent me to San Diego, California. After boot camp, they first assigned me to the USS *King DLG-10*. After that, I traveled to Japan and then the Philippines.

Following my stint in the navy, I started a successful landscaping business. I thought that once I'd returned to civilian life and had a good job, I could overcome my overwhelming need for alcohol and drugs.

I was totally ignorant of just how powerless I'd become, until one day, as I walked the streets of town, I saw a check for $42.50 lying in the gutter. I desperately wanted a beer, so I cashed the check.

Realizing I'd broken the law, I caught a bus for Florida. Before long I was picked up and brought back. I plea bargained for a three-year sentence in Texas. While I was being booked, I asked the officer, "What are you doing?"

"I'm looking for fleas and lice. Now turn around and . . ."

Before he could finish his sentence I told him, "I'm no dog!" Then I gave him a one-two punch in the mouth. As expected, I was instantly escorted to the hole.

After being in the hole for three days, a Gideon brought me a Bible. I threw it under my cot without giving it a thought.

Three weeks later, around midnight, the moon cast its light directly into my cell, shining right on the Bible poking out from beneath my cot. In spite of everything, God hadn't given up on me. Without hesitation I picked up my Bible and placed it on my bunk. I needed a friend, so I sat down and opened it up to John 3:16. After I read it, I fell on my knees and accepted Jesus as my Savior.

[EDITOR'S NOTE: *Jimmy Huff has a letter ministry and ministers in person to people in jails, prisons, and nursing homes. He may be contacted at Jimmy Huff Ministry, 130 West 6th Street, Colorado City, TX 79512.*]

❧ ☙

After we sincerely repent before the Lord, we must choose to walk in complete forgiveness from our heavenly Father—today, tomorrow, and every day—even though we continue to serve our sentences. No matter how small or large you think your idea is, let God use you by speaking out and using your hearts, gifts, and resources to bless others.

Michele Millikan
founder of *Prison Living Magazine*

THE IN SIDE by Matt Matteo

Reprinted by permission of Matt Matteo.

❧❧

I never really look for anything. What God throws my way comes. I wake up in the morning and whichever way God turns my feet, I go.

Pearl Bailey

Keep Your Balance, Nurture Your Spirit

TOM LAGANA AND LAURA LAGANA

5.1 Communicate with a higher power and nourish your spirit. Find a quiet place, at least ten to fifteen minutes, every day. Be still. Get in touch with your inner spirit and your Creator. Pray, meditate, practice yoga, Tai Chi, and so on. Do what is within your level of comfort. Anyone can do this. All you need is an open heart and peaceful mind.

5.2 What are your favorite prayers or sayings that connect you with your Maker?

5.3 Who do you pray for?

5.4 What do you pray for?

5.5 Write your own personal prayer. Be sure to include what you are thankful for and ask God for forgiveness.

5.6 Are there opportunities for you to pray in small groups?

5.7 Describe how respectful and tolerant you are of the spiritual beliefs of others.

5.8 Walk and meditate. Dan Millstein, founder of Visions for Prisons, suggests taking a walking meditation every day. Even lockdowns don't have to stop you. Pace back and forth, eight to twelve feet or even only a few steps. With each step become aware of your breathing. Walk for at least twenty minutes.

SIX

Changing from the Inside Out

Change is by far the hardest thing I have done.
It took years of being brutally honest with myself,
facing my demons, and seeing the monster I had
become in order to reach the point I am at today.
Many times along the way, I wanted to throw
in the towel and give up. I hated facing the
incomprehensible pain I had caused my family,
friends, and my victims. It was easier just to give
up, but I couldn't. I had too much at stake.

CHRISTOPHER BOWERS

The Person You Once Knew

BRIAN M. FISHER

I'm not the person
You once knew.
No longer, "The kid."
It's sad, but true.

Many years have passed
To begin anew.
I've changed my ways,
And you should too.

The boy I was
When I left that town
Sprang forth a man
Shackled and bound.

As for my debt,
I shall pay my due.
And keep mistakes
Far and few.

Next time we meet,
You might ask, "Who?"
For I'm not the person
You once knew . . .

Worthy of a Better Life

LAURIE E. STOLEN

Every day I'm reminded of my first day here. I was scared. I knew I had to be tough or I'd surely be eaten alive. After all, the movies I'd seen confirmed my belief that this place was filled with nothing but bad people who had done horrid things; it was jail, the clink, the big house, the slammer, with a bunch of hardened, tattooed, violent criminals locked up for their assorted crimes.

Movies are true, aren't they? Isn't this what everyone knows jail to be: dark, cold, dirty, stinking, violent, and noisy . . . a warehouse of convicts and worthless bums; people the rest of the world want to wash their hands of, or better yet, forget about?

The picture of this "inside" world isn't appealing. Anywhere you hear conversations about incarceration you hear it spoken in hushed tones or in shadows of shame. Very few ever get the chance to come inside. Unless you've worked in a jail or have been locked up in one, you hear only what the outside world wants you to know regarding what happens behind these walls. I'd like to set the record straight.

I was wrong and so are many others. How movies portray jail isn't anywhere near the truth of what happens behind these walls. This place is humane, clean, safe, and only noisy in the gymnasium during tight-scoring basketball games. The majority of people who fill the space between these walls, those who don't go home at the end of their shifts, are fathers, brothers, sons, and daughters. They are neighbors, coworkers, or even our relatives. Often they are people who get caught up with the wrong crowd, succumb to addictive behaviors, or have mental health issues for which they can't afford to seek treatment. They laugh and cry just like you and me.

I'm reminded of the day I performed a status check while giving a housing officer a lunch break. As I walked past each of the cells during premeal lockdown, to ensure the inmates were alive and breathing, I quickly glanced into each room to verify their status. When I came upon several inmates sleeping, an immediate sense of tranquillity came over me. One of them was curled up in the fetal position, sleeping soundly like a little child taking a nap. I thought to myself, *You are someone's child*. Then I wondered, *What was his childhood like?* I could only imagine that it may have been an unfulfilling time, perhaps cluttered with chaos, overshadowed with neglect and abuse. I also realized that not all inmates came from "bad" environments. Perhaps his formative years were the best years of his life, but somehow he got lost anyway.

I was simply a young kid who wanted a job. During my first weeks here, I acted like I didn't care about anyone or anything, and that was how I treated everyone around me. I refused to let anyone think I was intimidated or terrified, which I was. I came across as strict, mean, and cold. No one smiled at me, so I never smiled back. That was how I planned to survive. I was just there to do my job. Eight years ago, I knew little about those strangers called inmates.

I've learned so much since then and have come to know some of these strangers. I see things differently now. My hard shell has softened, and my intimidation has vanished. There's no need for it now.

I'm touched by the pain flowing through these walls. I hear their stories, and I can better understand. I see their tears and feel their pain. I listen to their dreams, and I want to help them come true. I want to make their lives better. I want them to enjoy life. I want them to love their children. I want them to know happiness and to taste success. This isn't a place filled with bad people.

The foundation of success is good character. No matter what road these people have traveled to get themselves here, they *can* change for the better and *never* come back. All they have to do is to know they can, and believe they're worthy of a better life. Every day I'm reminded of my first day here. I just didn't care then, but I do now.

🌿🌿

Become a possibilitarian. No matter how dark things seem to be or actually are, raise your sights and see possibilities; always see them, for they're always there.

Dr. Norman Vincent Peale

Reprinted by permission of Mark T. Pieczynski.

Parting Sorrow

SHAWN FOX

At age five or six, I started using drugs with my older brother and the drug dealer who lived in our camper in the backyard. From age eleven on, I was raised in boys' homes and cages as addiction took its natural progression from my early using to extremes. I can't remember really having fun or enjoying being high. It was just an escape, a numbing of the reality that was my life . . . anything to change the feelings or shut them off, even for just a few miserable hours. No matter how fast or far I ran, I couldn't get away from me! No matter where I went, there I was.

I'm a recovering addict and a member of the Narcotics Anonymous group inside the Oregon State Penitentiary. Today I've chosen to live my life clean, facing my problems and feelings head-on. What a relief that has turned out to be. I know God didn't design me to be high and disengaged from life.

Not long ago, my best bro and I were selected to interview each other for a public radio project: a collection of oral histories that were recorded all over the United States, aired on the radio and stored in the Library of Congress. My friend shared about his certainty that he would someday be released from this institution. Twenty-five days after our interview was played on the radio, my friend was found dead from an overdose on the floor of his cell.

This guy was a loving husband and father with thirteen children and twelve grandchildren. He had a larger-than-life persona and knew how to be a friend. If anyone needed help, he was always there. He was a gentle giant of a man. He started showing up at meetings, but his attendance was sporadic. I thank God we had enough of a program to love him no matter what. He had a lot of anger, shame, and despair in him. Sometimes he would talk about it, but he could not or *would* not work the steps.

My friend died of our disease, and not a day goes by that I don't miss him and feel the pain of this loss. My grief cuts deep. Every day I remember, *Whatever our circumstances, we don't have to end this way*.

[EDITOR'S NOTE: *For more information on Narcotics Anonymous World Services, Inc., contact P.O. Box 9999, Van Nuys, CA 91409; phone: 818-773-9999; website: www.na.org*.]

❧❧

> *Be careful the environment you choose for it will shape you; be careful the friends you choose for you will become like them.*
>
> W. Clement Stone

Greyhounds in Prison

MALEAH STRINGER

Reality set in when I arrived at Pendleton Correctional Facility. My objectives were to introduce Bella, my personal pet, so the staff and inmates could see and touch a greyhound, many for the first time, and also to see how Bella would respond to that particular setting.

I found it hard to ignore the razor wire and watchtowers, being searched, and doors that locked behind me. I had the ridiculous thought that once I got inside, they wouldn't let me out. Maybe I had seen too many movies.

The deeper I went into the prison, the more agitated I became. By the time I got to the cell block, I was almost a total wreck. There were probably 100 men on each side of me in general population, staring at Bella and me. My thought was, *Thank God I don't have to go down there*.

The next thing I heard was, "Are you ready?"

I was ready—ready to get out of there and go home. I started to walk out but quickly remembered the door was locked. I came close to screaming, "Let me out now," but somehow I managed to keep my mouth shut.

Then I heard the question a second time. "Are you ready to go into general population so the guys can see the dog?"

"You've got to be kidding me!" My tongue betrayed me.

Everyone looked at me. Someone responded, "No, Maleah, I'm not kidding you." So many thoughts ran through my head. I was scared out of my wits. *So what's it gonna be? What are you made of? I might as well be taking Bella straight down into hell with me.* My quivering knees almost buckled as I walked down the steps. I knew it wouldn't be in my best interest to look afraid, in case I came back. When they finally let me out that day, I wondered if I was capable of doing this program. I wasn't sure I had the guts.

When I told people about the program, they had multiple questions, such as, "Aren't you afraid the inmates will hurt the dogs?" I gave them an emphatic, "No, not at all." But deep in my heart I worried about the very same thing.

When we put the first group of dogs into the facility, I was a wreck for the first day or so. The next day I rushed to Pendleton to check on the dogs and make sure they were okay. As I walked in, I saw the inmates petting their dogs. Then I watched one of the greyhounds rub up against the legs of a huge, mean-looking man. Inside my head, I screamed, *No, don't go up to him.* Somehow I remained calm and stayed put, watching and waiting to see what would happen next. To my surprise, the man dropped to his knees and gently stroked the dog.

It has been several years now, and I've learned so much. Animals offer unconditional love, and I believe they carry a spark of the Divine. The inmates strive to overcome the shame and guilt of their addictions and step into the light. The gift of love from the greyhounds makes a positive difference in their recovery. It might be the only place these inmates receive unconditional love and forgiveness.

The Second Chance at Life Greyhound Prison Program is about second chances and rehabilitation. It's about not judging people. It's also about seeing the prisoners for who they are trying to be now . . . not who they used to be. I no longer worry about them hurting the dogs. Sometimes I think I'd rather leave them with the inmates than take a chance on putting them in homes. The greyhounds are bringing out the best in incarcerated men and women.

This program is bringing out the best in me as well. One of the guys at Pendleton once asked me, "Did you ever think you'd be sitting in a cell block with convicts and dogs?"

"Not in my wildest dreams," I said. "But life's funny. Sometimes you end up exactly where you're supposed to be."

[EDITOR'S NOTE: *For more information on the National Organization for Second Chance at Life Greyhound Prison Partnership, contact the National Greyhound Foundation, phone: 352-628-2281; e-mail: topdog@4greyhounds.org; website: www.4greyhounds.org/prison or www.IndyPrison Greyhounds.org.*]

Reprinted by permission of Charles Carkhuff.

The Road to Nowhere

DAVE LEFAVE

It's hard to stay focused and in touch with my dreams,
to block out the voices and misguiding screams.
They echo in my mind and tell me to escape . . .
attracting me to a world where everything is fake

Including my feelings and the dreams that I chased.
Now I'll always have memories of years gone to waste
I buried my feelings and blocked out all pain . . .
Acknowledging the sunshine while ignoring the rain.

I'm fooled into believing things are just fine . . .
and everybody's life is as carefree as mine.
Actually the pain just gets bottled inside . . .
and it slowly eats at my morals and pride.

I can see what I'm doing and the need for a change . . .
Yet suddenly stopping is both scary and strange.
I know it's for the best and it needs to be done . . .
that life is more than parties and always having fun.

These things are fine at the right time and right place
but I never seem able to stop giving chase.
I lose all control and keep one thing in mind . . .
and from the direction I travel, you'd swear I was blind.

I've repeated this pattern more times than you know . . .
and the price I keep paying is starting to show.
I'm certainly not proud of the road that I took . . .
I labeled myself as a liar and crook.

My future meant nothing, I lived for each day . . .
rebelling against authority and all they would say.
I thought I knew it all and I was so cool . . .
but looking at my past, I see the life of a fool.

I'm older now, but I still hear that voice.
The difference is I can see there's a choice
I've learned a lesson that can't be found in a book . . .
and that's to stay off the road that I took.

It leads to nowhere, I've learned firsthand . . .
as the direction I traveled was not what I planned.

*I don't know what God has planned for my life after my
release, but I know this time I will listen to His voice.*

Christopher Bowers

Con Artists

LEONARD BAYLIS

The painting was crude. The lighthouse leaned to the right, the colors blurred together, and the ocean looked more like a pond. Mark stood before it, brush in hand, admiring it proudly with a faraway look in his eyes as if he were a part of the scene; the sun at his back, absorbing the ocean air, mesmerized by the movement of the surf curling and crashing before slipping quietly back into the ocean in a whisper.

I glance over at *my* work, a blazing orange sunset with two black shadows in the foreground that were supposed to be horses—one with a rider, the other trailing behind. Two sheepdogs trot along at a distance. I'm inexperienced, and my picture isn't done very well, but I can see the scene clearly in my mind: the mountains of Virginia surrounded by incredible vistas, appreciating how small I really am in the scheme of things.

As I gaze at my work of art, I feel the heat of the horse's body beneath me as I ride and the rocking motion of his gait. Along the Appalachian Trail, I approach a path dense with trees. Dappled light animates the rocks and tree trunks with moving patterns. I hear a stream dancing and laughing nearby.

Suddenly I pull myself back to the present, here in the class of the prison arts program, bars on the windows, before I get an "escape charge." Some of us are learning how to create instead of destroy.

One of my challenges is attention deficit disorder,

commonly referred to as ADD. I make simple mistakes, am easily distracted by extraneous stimuli, and have difficulty following through on instructions. I have problems organizing tasks, and I either forget things or lose them altogether.

Before I get them right, I must do things over and over again; just thinking about it makes me tired, especially when I consider how many times I've gotten into trouble with the law and life in general. Purposeful activities, such as drawing, painting, and writing, help me negotiate the formidable force of my experience and communicate it in a positive way.

Mark is short-tempered and is often depressed. Since working in the art program, he has a better handle on things. There he stands, a paintbrush instead of a weapon in his right hand, his left hand relaxed, not balled up into a fist, and his brow calm and smooth rather than creased with tension and distrust.

I can't imagine what the group of us might look like to outsiders, two supposedly hardened criminals painting pictures. I'm sure many people may scoff at the idea of an art program inside a prison. To understand it, they would have to be here to see a man, once unable to stay focused on one thing, accomplish something tangible through art.

At present our artwork may be merely fledgling efforts, but we're interested enough to improve our capabilities and our lives. We have also found a way to journey to a better place legally—a worthy process in these troubled times, both in here and out in the free world.

Our greatest glory is not in never falling, but in rising every time we fall.

Confucius

Insight from the Inside Out—A to Z

TOM LAGANA AND LAURA LAGANA

"Using only one sentence, what would you say to someone that might keep them from going to prison?"

As we conduct programs and interact with inmates throughout the United States, in what typically become intense and perceptive sessions, this question yields some attention-grabbing reactions. During this exercise, we usually follow up with: "While you ponder your answer, visualize your words inspiring another person to change their behavior and keep them from getting into trouble."

Much of the following enlightened feedback may well apply to anyone, whether inside or outside the confines of prison.

Appreciate what you have.

Be your own person.

Choose your friends carefully.

Don't follow the crowd.

Expect to work brutally hard at following the letter of the law.

Face your problems and issues.

Get your life right.

Have faith and rest assured no one can take that from you.

Include good and positive people in your life.

Just do your best and live free from drugs, today and forever.

Know thyself.

Learn from your mistakes.

Make positive adjustments.

Never give up.

Offer to help, and don't be afraid to ask for it when you
need it.

Put your pain and pride aside when you've messed up, seek
forgiveness, then make amends.

Quit doing negative things that will lead to jail.

Resist the temptation to revert to negative behaviors.

Stay sober, get a job, and go to school.

Take a good hard look at yourself and what you're becoming.

Use good judgment.

Value your life while you can.

Watch out for anyone who tries to stop you from accom-
plishing your goals.

Xtra attention to learning all you can paves the way to a
promising future.

You are worth more than you allow yourself to be.

Zip your lips when you're tempted to say something you
might regret.

*I hated what I had done with my life. I hated prison and
set it in stone and in my heart that I would never return
to prison.*

Brian Brookheart
author of *A Prisoner: Released*
and *The Ten Best Days of My Life*

Changed

NOLAN P. HOLLIDAY

I was walking up and down South Broadway one day.
Hustlin' in the streets out in downtown L.A.

I was hooked on heroin, cocaine, and booze,
Knowing that this fight I would certainly lose.

You see, I told lies to many, stole from some,
I hate to reflect on certain things I've done.

But this day was different, as I soon did see,
When I met an old friend who was once like me.

His life had been changed, that I truly found out,
From his speech and appearance there was no doubt.

"What happened to you?" I asked with a sincere look,
So he reached in his pocket and took out a "Book."

"It was God," he said. "I'm out of that game."
Since that day, I've also been changed!

*Every tomorrow has two handles. We can take hold of
it with the handle of anxiety or the handle of faith.*

Henry Ward Beecher

Free as a Bird

CHARLES T. FEHIL

Many inmates rationalize they're in prison because of an addiction. As for me, I couldn't explain why I got caught in the "revolving door" of prison, so to justify my actions, I played with meth. It just made it easier for me to say, "I'm an addict," than to admit that I'd already given up on myself.

I had an awful childhood. My mother was abusive and my father, one of her victims, would *go to the store* for hours to avoid her reign of terror, leaving his children alone with the monster under our beds—mental and physical pain.

My mother told me over and over, "You're a loser and a failure. You'll never amount to anything." She repeated it so many times that eventually I fulfilled her expectations. Prison was my only refuge.

Once I was asked, "What does recovery mean to you?" Now that I'm an "addict in recovery," I was instructed to write an essay on the subject. I didn't have an answer to that question, but it got me to revisit my childhood and my dad.

I don't recall my dad ever taking me to Little League practice. I don't remember him telling me about the birds and bees, but Mom showed me in her own unique way. I can't recall Dad teaching me to drive, but I do remember one event.

I was about seven. Our house had an enclosed porch. Somehow a bird got in there and couldn't get out. To me this was one of the coolest things, but it annoyed my dad. The bird flapped against the window, attempting to get out. I couldn't stop laughing. That bird flew from one window to another, banging into each one with a thud. Each time I opened a window, that darn bird flew into another one that was closed. After I'd opened every window, that poor creature focused on the door.

"Look, stupid bird," I shouted, "I'm trying to help you!" I guess that bullheaded bird was dead-set against any help. My dad said, "Just leave the windows open. He'll find his way out." When we came back later, we found the bird, lying lifeless on the floor next to the door, even though all eight windows were open.

Now, thirty years later, I still can't figure out why that bird wouldn't let me help. I wasn't going to hurt him. He wanted to find freedom all by himself, so he died trying. Reminds me of someone I know.

So, getting back to that question, "What does recovery mean to you?" it means not being like that stupid bird. I spent too many years not trusting people, going from an open window to one that was closed—not having the ability to open it on my own, yet not daring to let someone open it for me; and when they did, I'd question their motives.

Now that I'm older and wiser, I see this in a new light. There is probably some scientific basis for the bird's behavior, but I prefer my interpretation. I know that I have a father who hasn't given up on me. Recently I've begun to accept his help. Unlike that foolish creature, I want to stand at the threshold of that closed door, shove it open, and walk out into the warm sunlight, free as a bird.

Hold fast to dreams, for if dreams die, life is a broken bird that cannot fly.

Langston Hughes

THE IN SIDE by Matt Matteo

Reprinted by permission of Matt Matteo.

The last of the human freedoms: to choose one's attitude in any given set of circumstances, to choose one's own way.

Viktor Frankl

Chart Your Course, Set Your Goals, Transform Your Life

TOM LAGANA AND LAURA LAGANA

6.1 Close your eyes and visualize your first day of freedom. What do you see? How do you feel? Who is with you? Where do you see yourself going? What do you smell? What can you taste? Be aware of the sounds that surround you. Are you doing things that will keep you out of trouble? If you don't like what you see, know that you have the freedom to see good things in your life, so change your thoughts and better results will follow.

6.2 List what you want out of life. On a separate piece of paper, list your goals. Be specific and include what you are willing to do in order to earn and keep your freedom. Think of goals as a guide or road map for your journey through life. Focus on all areas, including:

    a. Family and relationships
    b. Job, career, and business
    c. Financial
    d. Spiritual
    e. Health and appearance
    f. Personal development
    g. Social life
    h. Humanitarian and making a difference
    i. Travel, hobbies, and entertainment

6.3 What can you do to make constructive changes in your life?

6.4 Write a 300-word essay on the following: "If I had my life to live over, I would . . ."

SEVEN

Stumbling Blocks to Stepping-stones

Isn't it strange that princesses and kings,
And clowns that caper in sawdust rings,
And everyday people like you and me,
Are builders of eternity?
Each is given a bag of tools;
A shapeless mass, a book of rules.
And each must make, 'ere life is flown,
A stumbling block or a stepping-stone.

R I. SHARPE

I'm Free

ALLISON "TAMMY" BUTLER

Not too long ago, I placed little value on my freedom, like the old saying, "You don't miss a good thing until it's gone." That's why it was so easy for me to trade it. Prison was designed to be a deterrent for the lifestyle I'd become accustomed to—my way of life.

Today I'm confined to prison walls I can see, the reality of man-made limitations I can measure. I'm engulfed in loneliness, indescribable loneliness. I've lost all control of my life, what fraction of it I still possess. I've been reduced to life's simplest form, sometimes being considered less than a person. Every day I'm reminded that I've lost control over mere decisions, like when to get up, when to take a shower, and for how long. I'm told when to go to meals, where to sit, and I no longer eat to enjoy but out of necessity. I can't decide who or when I may talk with someone, and uniformed officers control the volume and tone of my voice.

Each day is the same as the day before—a new world for me to experience, one in which everyone is the same. We dress alike, eat the same foods, and share the same misgivings. I'm in a place overpopulated with people who no longer hide behind emotions and failing expectations. I'm in a place where I'm not allowed to make simple choices. I have to live by rules that are simple in more ways than one. I'm surrounded by hundreds who are bound by the same chains of unfulfilled goals and dissolving dreams. I'm in a place where

I merely exist as a case, a blue file, an assigned number forced to cope with the solitude—forced to cope with what I've lost. It doesn't matter if I don't know what to do. Someone will tell me. After all, I've proven to the world that I'm incapable of making it on my own. I had my chance. I gave it up. It was my foreseeable end.

Now I tremble with fear because I'm comfortable. My friends and family are disturbed by my cheery attitude, my smile when I should be depressed at my destruction, my laughter, some of which is the best I've ever experienced—when I should be crying at the devastation I've created for myself, my family, and my children.

Shocked by my own attitude, I lay on my bottom bunk and stare at my surroundings: my cramped living quarters, my pictures fixed to the cabinet with toothpaste, my bar of bright yellow state-issued hand soap that rests on a sanitary napkin wrapped in light pink as my soap dish. The cluttered stainless steel table and stools hold borrowed books, *Chicken Soup for the Prisoner's Soul,* and a Bible. My brown cardboard box with a lid, marked Allison Butler OL8397, contains all I own, all someone else decided I could possess, limiting what I can take with me from one place to another. Anything I can't fit into the box, I can't have.

My life has been greatly simplified—no people to impress, no one to lie to, no one to disappoint, and no struggle to be who I was expected to be. I'm free—still confined, committed to the State of Pennsylvania Department of Corrections. I'm free—free from my temptations, selfishness, and the pressure to have what my neighbor has; free from my condition of life, my holding pattern; free from my mind, my fear of being exposed; free to serve while serving time; free to tell the truth, to feel the consequences, to grow and heal slowly, permanently; free to be well, whole, responsible; free to forget the past, forgive myself for my failures; free to develop patience through pain, to live in the reality of today, not yesterday or tomorrow; free to develop a positive outcome, to know myself for me in spite of me, to be weak, to spend time with the brokenhearted, the stripped, the beaten, and abandoned; free to learn true compassion.

Freedom is welcoming confinement between four walls in exchange for an escape plan from my self-imposed prison. Freedom is power . . . power to change. The cost of my freedom was giving it up. Don't misunderstand. Just like most people, I want to be home, out of this physical prison. I recognize that without it, the process of the power to change would be hindered. Without this mandatory opportunity, there would have been no time for self-evaluation, no place to cover old wounds with immoral and criminal actions. I would still be working hard at being "better than" instead of "better for." There would have been no real gratitude or reflection on what God's grace is like, no true appreciation for my life exactly as it is and understanding of how to cast off my cares. I couldn't love who God created me to be or see great opportunities from my past and my pain. I now have time to focus on my salvation.

❧ ❧

One who gains strength by overcoming obstacles possesses the only strength which can overcome adversity.
Albert Schweitzer

THE IN SIDE by Matt Matteo

THE VALUE OF EARPLUGS....
PRICELESS.

Reprinted by permission of Matt Matteo.

To every disadvantage there is a corresponding advantage.
W. Clement Stone

Reading 101

ROSE M. ROBACKER

As a seventy-year-old teacher, I knew I needed to get out of the classroom. I also understood that, because I loved teaching, that's all I really wanted to continue to do. The Adult Literacy Program was perfect for me. When I first began my fifteen hours of training, I didn't have the foggiest idea how to begin teaching an adult to read, let alone people whose second language was English. Soon I learned that anyone who can read, and especially anyone who loves to read, could indeed teach someone else to read by using the Laubach program.

I barely had time to get my feet wet as a volunteer when the program director asked me to run the program in the local county jail. I had never been inside a jail. I had no idea whether I could handle that type of student or if I would feel threatened, but I agreed to try it.

My background as a Catholic nun, a principal of several schools, and a teacher of chemistry and math for forty-seven years had not really prepared me for this endeavor.

One sixty-three-year-old man could not read a single letter of the alphabet when we began. He was bright and a very hard worker—truly a delight. We completed book one and had nearly completed book two. He was so happy to be able to read. His thanks at the end of each class was a real lift. He told me that each morning he would get up before the other guys in his cell, read book one in its entirety before going through book two, and then move along to the flash cards.

One day when I called for him as my next student, the warden stared at me. "Rose," he said. "I'm sorry, but Harry died yesterday. He suffered a heart attack." I almost broke into tears. He was a sweet man. When I returned home, I told my husband about Harry, saying that now it didn't matter to him that he had been unable to read. Bob wisely replied, "Oh, but it did when he was alive. What a difference you made in his life."

Another man in his late fifties had taught himself to read a blueprint but nothing more. He was a construction worker and had toiled on the Twin Towers in New York City. Since he was very bright, we sailed through the introductory books, and soon he was reading well. One day, I asked him why he had never learned to read since he was an excellent student. His reply stunned me to the core, especially since I had been a teacher.

"Rose, I'll tell you why I can't read. I grew up in Brooklyn forty years ago and must have been a hellion in the first grade because they put me in a special class. Not special ed classes as we know them today, but a class for those who couldn't behave in a regular classroom. For three or four years, we had a male teacher who came in each morning, took roll, and then went to the faculty room. At the end of the day, he came back to dismiss us." By this time I was genuinely upset. I asked him what he had learned. He said he learned to defend himself. Imagine! His entire class lost out. When I heard this story, I was almost ashamed that I had been a teacher.

One exceptionally bright man was working hard to get his GED. I told him that he would need the fifty-dollar fee required by the local school that administers the test. He said, "I'll get it from my father in California." A few weeks later, the warden came down to my teaching area to give him a letter from California, thinking it was the fee money. When the young man opened it, he looked stunned. He told me it was from his mother, whom he had not heard from nor seen for many years. He waited to read her letter when he got back to his cell.

Weeks later, he asked me if I remembered the letter he had received from his mother. He had no idea how to respond to her letter in which she blamed herself for his taking the wrong path in life. He had decided to write a loving poem for his mother and sent it to her.

A few years ago, two young men held up a bank teller in the local grocery store at gunpoint. Then they foolishly bought a car, paid for it in cash, and ended up in our jail. Since they were last-semester seniors at a nearby school, and each needed only seven additional credits for graduation, they wanted to try for their diplomas. That's where I stepped in. I think I learned more than they did, because my science/math background did not prepare me for teaching literature, social studies, technical writing, and health. The teachers at their school were extremely helpful, giving me their curricula and some tests and such to guide me. With much struggle on all sides, the two young men graduated, and the jail held a ceremony at which we presented the diplomas—truly a rewarding experience.

On another occasion I was coming back up to the main floor from the basement of the jail where I tutor. I usually start teaching around 7:30 AM and work until about 3:00 PM. This particular day it was approximately 3:00 PM, and I was thirsty and hungry and not paying close attention to what I was doing. With a briefcase in one hand and my coat in the other, I missed a step and fell forward, landing hard on the cement landing and hitting my jaw. Besides a black-and-blue jaw, I had also split my lip. Lip injuries bleed profusely and everyone was concerned. The corrections officers (COs) applied ice to my lip and then decided it would be wise to take me to the local hospital. I didn't want to go, but they won out, so two officers escorted me to the emergency room in their police car.

At the time I didn't understand why the emergency room staff looked at me so strangely. Later, when I thought more about it, I figured they probably wondered what an old lady had done to be put in jail and to engage in a fight to boot. The guards stayed right with me, even when I had to go back to the gurney for a tetanus shot. By the time I figured this out, it hurt too much to laugh, so I chuckled about it inside.

It has been more than fifteen years since I agreed to try volunteering in the jail. Teaching about twenty men to read and helping more than two hundred others to earn their GEDs has been the most challenging and satisfying undertaking of my life.

[EDITOR'S NOTE: *Laubach Literacy Action and Literacy Volunteers of America merged in 2000 to create ProLiteracy Worldwide. For information, contact 1320 Jamesville Avenue, Syracuse, NY 13210; e-mail: info@proliteracy.org; website: www.proliteracy.org; phone: 315-422-9121.*]

❧

Having hired many ex-felons, I have found them to be some of the most outstanding citizens, competent workers, and excellent employees. So, we need to be careful about making judgments of people until we get to know who they really are. "You can't tell a book by its cover." You have to read it in order to know it well.

Dave E. Ritzenthaler

A Puddle and a Prayer

MICHAEL CHERNOCK

It was a static-filled day—the kind that starts with an alarm clock that fails to ring, a broken shoelace, and just enough gas in the car to make it to the first gas station. On top of all this, you end up running late for everything for the rest of the day.

This is how it was when I arrived behind schedule at San Quentin State Prison one Sunday. It was my day for conducting church services in the HIV ward. By the time I got there, I was met with a series of countless delays and frustrations that postponed me from ministering to my flock.

Following the service, one of the long-term residents asked me if I was an ordained priest. I'd been asked this question a number of times, and as a proponent of "walk your talk," I'm well aware of the importance of maintaining credibility by being honest and up front with the residents. I explained, "I'm actually a lay volunteer, but I uphold the rules, rites, and regulations as set forth by the prison and my boss, the chaplain." My tone must have revealed the kind of day I was having because I concluded my explanation with a slight hint of irritation and the words, "Is that what you wanted to know?"

My friend in the orange jumpsuit smiled. I suspect he'd experienced more than his fair share of static-laden days of his own. Planting his huge, firm hand on my shoulder he said, "What I wanted to know is, will you baptize me?"

Performing baptisms has always been a common part of our

services, but in the decade I've been engaged in this ministry, no single baptism has ever been "common." Any of God's servants who have been granted the privilege of bringing a willing soul into the family of God knows it's always as special a day for the baptizer as it is for the baptized.

Shaking with excitement, I tried to look cool and collected. Fumbling open the hasps on the communion box, I reached for the bottle of Jordan River water that I always carried for such occasions. That's when I discovered that I had removed it for a grandchild's baptism and had forgotten to return it. In a panic, I looked around. The only water nearby was left over from the previous night's rain in a muddy puddle at my feet. Hoping the French philosopher Voltaire was right when he said, "God has a sense of humor," I secretly scooped a small amount of puddle water into the communion cup. As I looked up I saw two orange suited gentlemen glaring at me.

Since they already thought I was incompetent, there was little left to do but cowboy up and complete my task. The baptism was an incredible event. As I filled out and signed the formal papers, the two men who had caught me collecting puddle water approached. I fully expected a severe dressing-down for my offensiveness and was ready with a dozen equally poor excuses. Instead they said, "We saw what you did, and we would like you to baptize us too—in the same water." They smiled knowingly, as if we had just shared a private joke.

❧ ❧

Like the saying goes "You hit bottom when you quit digging." By the grace of God, prison was the place where I was able to set my shovel down and leave it behind when I left.

Kurt R. Mosher

Learning to Trust

DAVID J. FEDDES

Our plates were loaded with bacon, eggs, hash browns, and toast as we shared breakfast and enlightening conversation at a nearby restaurant. My companions were seven Christian men who had been released from prison within the past five years and a few mentors from local churches. As we ate, we talked and laughed about a variety of things. Then I asked a serious question. "What was the hardest thing for you guys when you got out of prison?"

One spoke up immediately. "Trust," he said. "The hardest thing was to trust anybody." The others nodded.

For some people, trust becomes difficult from an early age. A child learns not to rely on a mother who is addicted to drink or drugs or a father who abuses or abandons his family. For these children, parental promises prove hollow. Without trustworthy parents, they tend to grow up relying on their own wits, not trusting parents or authorities.

Without trust or respect for authority, it's a small step to crime and prison, and there trust is unlikely to flourish. Correctional officers and officials often mistrust people who are convicted lawbreakers. People in prison mistrust each other, often with good reason. In many cases, any remaining ties with family members or friends on the outside are broken after a person is locked up. As a release date approaches, people feel they will be unwelcome and distrusted anywhere they go. Experiencing prison tends to harden the habit of not trusting others. It also strengthens the impression that others don't trust you and would rather have nothing to do with you. If anyone does show interest in you, there must be a hidden agenda.

Without trust, healthy relationships cannot grow. But without healthy relationships, trust cannot grow. It's a vicious cycle but not an unbreakable one.

Around the breakfast table that morning were men who had found trust to be the hardest thing. Yet somehow trust had come to life and had grown in their hearts. At the deepest level, the source of their growing trust was God's grace in a Savior who died for them, touching their hearts through the presence of the Holy Spirit.

But this did not happen in a vacuum. For some, trust began to grow when a godly chaplain showed genuine care and taught God's trustworthy Word. Christian visitors from outside the prison joined the men inside during worship times, and upon release the men found it easier to trust these faithful, familiar visitors rather than complete strangers.

Trust also grows through lessons and letters from volunteers. Bible lessons reveal a heavenly Father whose love never fails, and every word can foster a greater capacity to trust.

[EDITOR'S NOTE: *To request an application for a free Bible study correspondence course and faith-based reentry program, contact Crossroad Bible Institute, P.O. Box 900, Grand Rapids, MI 49509-0900; website: www.crossroadbible.org.*]

Being with God does not eliminate life's struggles. Sharing can give others a feeling of normality through the sharing of life's struggles, and a sense that God is with the one who struggles as much as the one who doesn't.

James Guy

It Starts with Trust

PATRICK MIDDLETON

When I was a teen, my grandfather would often remind me to choose my friends carefully. I never did though. I had one real friend, and he chose me. I was a delinquent, whereas he was an upstanding boy. Throughout all my skull-duggeries, my friend was there for me—never embarrassed, never judging, never giving up on me. Forty years later, he's an engineer, I'm a seasoned convict, and we're still friends. There's a lesson here. It has to do with loyalty.

Prison has taught me some precious lessons about life. I've learned, for example, that there are two distinct worlds in which we humans live—the internal and the external. Each has its boundaries of freedom. My external world now consists of the walkways and hallways, the prison yard, the chapel, other buildings, and this little room of a cell. There is much more freedom, though, in my inner world. The walk-ways can lead to just about anywhere, and I am free to believe. I am free to believe in a God or none at all. I can choose alge-bra or geometry. I can see the glass as half empty or half full, and if I wish, I can cultivate love and goodwill in the hearts and minds of others and my own.

There are also lessons about friendship. How life is so much better when we have a few good friends to share it with. It takes time, sometimes years, to cultivate lasting friendships. It starts with trust. We take chances, we show our vulnerabilities, and it's a beautiful thing when it's reciprocated. Along the way, we learn to listen and encourage, we share our histories, our hills and valleys, we laugh and tease and sometimes cry together, and so much more.

Many of the friends I've gained over the years are fellow musicians. We worked hard together. We argued, fussed, and created lots of good music and many special memories. We grew as musicians and as human beings. We came to depend on each other for a smile or an ear when we needed it. There was a spiritual comfort in knowing they had my back, and I had theirs.

What do you do after you've shared years of your life with a friend who is suddenly transferred or goes home or dies? How do you deal with that "missing you" feeling, that homesick feeling you felt when you first came to prison?

We stay strong. We wait for time to lessen the pain. We work on new friendships, and from time to time, we rearrange the pictures of our friends in our photo albums. We relive the memories of them in our minds, and if that's not enough, we talk to our old friends when we're alone. We tell them how much we miss them and remember that in having known them, life has been good to us.

My incarceration has taught me to never take life for granted and to appreciate everything in life, especially family and friends.

Mark T. Pieczynski

It's Never Too Late

SUE ELLEN ALLEN

"It's never too late." I've often said that to others, but I wasn't including myself. At age fifty-seven and facing countless firsts, I thought it was too late for me. This was my first time in prison, first time with cancer, first time to lose a breast, first chemo, and first radiation. The idea of "life" held terror for me. What could I possibly hope for now except peaceful oblivion?

When I went from jail to the hospital for my mastectomy, I engaged in a one-sided conversation with God. "This would be a really good time to take me home, Lord. Right there on the table, one slip, and I could see the light at the end of the tunnel. I'm ready, but if I wake up, I'll know You aren't done with me yet." About five hours later I did wake up, and even in my drugged state, I got the message. Realizing I was still alive, I thought, *Oh dear, God has other plans*.

Now, when I walk across the prison yard to my math class and feel the sun on my face, I'm thankful to be alive and on my way to face fractions. I haven't had math in forty years. Back then, math was not my friend. I fought it every step of the way. I passed, but I hated it.

Here in prison, I passed the mandatory math tests at the ninth-grade level, but I have an opportunity to be tutored to raise my score and learn those pesky fractions, percentages, algebra, and geometry. In forty years of living since high school, I've learned that math is useful, and I like exercising my brain.

The worst thing about prison isn't the lack of privacy, awful food, or petty rules. It's the huge waste of minds—so many inmates and not enough money to provide classes or jobs for all of them. So, mostly they lay on their bunks, reading volumes of romance novels or watching TV, if they have one—not their first preference. Most of them would prefer to work or go to school, but since neither is available, they waste their time. And when they are released, they have no preparation for the outside world.

Most of them are young, and their crimes are drug related. It seems to me most are addicts needing treatment, but the state puts them here—where they meet more addicts, more users, and more sellers—not the best atmosphere for "going straight." There's not enough money for other options, so the cycle continues and society continues to pay. Prison is expensive rehab.

Many of these women at twenty-four, thirty-four, or even forty-four think it's already too late for them. But if I can believe it's not too late for me at fifty-seven, then I can reflect that back to them. God has given us life. The state has given us time. We can do good time, bad time, or waste time. The best we can do is *use* this time to grow spiritually, mentally, and physically. We can exercise, pray, read our Bibles, and study self-help books. Then we can start making a difference.

By the way, I took my math test and scored at the twelfth-grade level, the highest possible. No matter what our age, if we have the determination and hope, it's never too late—inside or out.

We often struggle with the bad things that come into our lives—the tragedies and things that knock us down. It is in these areas that we struggle to see how they can make us better people and how we can grow from them.

Troy Evans

THE IN SIDE by Matt Matteo

Reprinted by permission of Matt Matteo.

Stay away from drugs and the gambling scene. If you are still on speaking terms with your family, keep in contact with them and prove to them you are working hard to get back with them as soon as possible. You're of no help to them in prison. A lot of it has to do with how much you're willing to work to stay "charge free" and maintain a positive attitude.

Rod Carter

Just a Tear

STEVEN D. GAUB

Pablo reminds me of the quintessential Los Angeles gang-banger. He is shorter than I am, so he caught my eye right away—a hard character but still quite young. A baby-faced Latin man who cut a hard stance, looking tougher than you could imagine. Tattoos covered his hands, forearms, and neck—even his face. There were so many symbols that I couldn't even guess their meaning.

I suspect that being so young-looking and small could be a real trial. This is a tight-security prison where the bad actors are sent when they get into trouble at a different facility. Many of them pump iron and build visual walls of hardness and swagger to keep themselves safe. It was said that the gang became Pablo's only family after he was rejected by his relatives. He was rumored to be the leader of the Crypt gang in prison. His snarl and evil eye told me I didn't want to meet him in a dark corner.

Kairos is a Christian prison ministry that strives to improve the environment. Volunteers from various Christian denominations serve the inmates by putting on a three-day religious retreat in the prison. The retreat includes fellowship, unconditional love, food, music, and short talks about basic Christianity. The most important aspect of Kairos is that its volunteers return to the prison every month for fellowship and "share and prayer" groups.

Kairos is designed to help melt the heart of just such a man as Pablo, and I suspect the prison chaplain had chosen Pablo because of his great need. After our time with the inmates in the evenings, I would hear from the other team members that Pablo was showing signs of progress. By the end of the weekend, he appeared to be more receptive to the Christian life, and I believe he even went to confession.

Pablo helped out with the weekend retreat in the spring for a new group of participants, scrubbing tables and making coffee. He led other inmates in the menial but essential behind-the-scenes work. He is always there for the monthly reunions and encourages his peers to preserve and live the Christian life—not an easy undertaking in prison. Whenever I return, I hear good things from the graduates and other inmates about how Pablo has changed.

Now one year later, Pablo is present at every Kairos function. In fact, he was selected for a leadership role. The last time I saw him he told me, "I wrote a letter to my family, confessing my sins and asking them to forgive me." He also mentioned that he had talked to his mother on the phone—the first time she had heard from him in years.

One of Pablo's gang tattoos is of a teardrop falling from the corner of one eye. I've heard that in gang symbolism, a tear represents someone he murdered. To have been part of the salvation and early rehabilitation of this man is a gift and a blessing far greater than anything I can imagine.

[EDITOR'S NOTE: *For information on Kairos Prison Ministry International, see website: www.kpmi.org; write to 6903 University Blvd., Winter Park, FL 32792; or phone: 407-629-4948.*]

A Unique Request

SCOTT PAUL-BONHAM

Lent is a busy time for a prison chaplain. Every spring there are special services to arrange and conduct for different religious groups. One year during Lent, an inmate asked me a unique question. "Chaplain, could you give me thirty minutes of your time so I can vent? I'm so full of hate and rage that if I don't let it out, I'll explode!"

This irritable inmate didn't normally attend chapel services, but he seemed to feel safe sharing his thoughts and feelings with me. I told him the required line, "I can keep what you say to me in confidence, as long as you don't make any statement threatening the safety and security of any person or the institution." He agreed, and we set a time.

As the appointed time approached, I arranged my office with two chairs facing each other without any desk or barrier between them. He arrived on time, and I shut the door. He sat. Then I sat. I prepared myself to play the "good chaplain" and let the man vent. I would listen and try to be attentive.

"You have bombed innocent Iraqi children! The blood from their severed and broken bodies is on your hands! Their parents scream in grief at you and demand to know why?" His words flooded out of him with incredible vehemence.

I was dumbfounded. The Iraq war had just begun a few days before. I had never been in the military, bombed, severed, or killed anyone. The inmate continued his tirade. He kept saying, "You, you, you," interjecting every dastardly thing the

United States had ever done or been accused of. "You lock up thousands of innocent people and throw away the key. You perpetuate slavery!"

Like coming out of a fog bank, it began to dawn on me. As a government employee, working for the Federal Bureau of Prisons, I was being personified as the United States government in this inmate's mind. The minutes slowly ticked by. For this stricken man, I became personally responsible for every perceived or actual act of stupidity or cruelty ever wrought by our government. As I was criticized, the bile rose up from my entrails into my chest and then my throat. My joints ached. I had not agreed to this.

I was nearing the point where I could take it no more. I was about to order the inmate to shut up and get out of my office, when the intensity of his accusations began to lighten. His speech became less shrill. His breathing calmed. "Thanks, Chaplain. I feel much better." It appeared that he spoke the truth. He left my office buoyant while I scrambled to find some antacid.

A few days later on Good Friday, I realized this man had given me a gift. I had a new understanding of Jesus's suffering on the cross. One man's half hour of venting had almost undone me physically, mentally, and spiritually. That Easter Sunday, I experienced a gratitude for God's gift of redemption in Christ that I pray I'll never lose.

❧ ❧

Too often we underestimate the power of a touch, a smile, a kind word, a listening ear, an honest compliment, or the smallest act of caring, all of which have the potential to turn a life around.

Leo Buscaglia

Stones

LEONARD BAYLIS

A stone wall—
Coarse, gray, looming—
A man, confined
Imagining:

The morning sky,
A city high-rise:
Steel, glass, and
Crushed stone;

A stone path
Through autumn woods,
Children playing brightly
Amid blazing leaves;
A wide river
A stone bridge
Crossing what was once impossible
To cross . . .

Stones:
Stones to build a city,
Stones to firm the earth,
Stones to cross the widest divide—
So much more to do with stones than build walls . . .

Launch Yourself to Success, Commit to Improvement

TOM LAGANA AND LAURA LAGANA

7.1 Make a list of what you will do to remain free in the future. Commit to continual self-improvement to become better every day.

7.2 Create an action plan. What will you commit to doing for continual improvement and success in life? What can you do today? What can you do this week and next month? What about next year? Be sure to focus on actions that could make a significant, positive impact on the various aspects of your life.

7.3 Commit to your action plan by writing it down; be specific and make sure it is measurable and realistic, with corresponding dates and times for each action. If you are dependent on others to achieve your goal, obtain their agreement. Make a contract with yourself. Sign and date it. Ask someone to witness your contract and help keep you accountable.

7.4 Pass it on. Share what you have learned and teach it to your peers and loved ones. This will help you internalize the information. Who will you share this with?

7.5 Celebrate your successes. Make a list of what you want to do (legally, of course) to celebrate your successes along the way, and then enjoy them, and enjoy life as a productive and free member of our society.

EIGHT

Discovering a Meaningful Purpose

After spending most of my life in prison, it
became clear to me that change was needed.
I had worked long and hard to change myself;
through this process I became convinced that
I had an obligation to work for the betterment
of the world I inhabit.

KENNETH E. HARTMAN

Giving a Life Back

TEKLA DENNISON MILLER

After retiring from corrections, I began writing. It opened up a rewarding world, but not a moneymaking venture. I write because I hope what I say will make my readers laugh, cry, touch their soul in a way they never thought possible, and maybe even change their lives.

Letters I receive from readers affirm the reason I write. One came from a former female gang member. Someone gave her my first memoir, *The Warden Wore Pink*. After reading it, she decided to go to college. Now she works with troubled youth and attributes her life change to reading the memoir. Another letter came from a teenager who was on house arrest when she heard me talk to the street law class at our local high school. Afterward, she read both my memoirs. She is now studying criminal justice.

Yet nothing prepared me for the call I received from Jeff. His story brought me to my knees. At the age of seventeen, Jeff was found guilty and sentenced to prison for fifteen years to life based on a coerced confession of the rape and murder of a schoolmate. After sixteen years in prison, Jeff had exhausted all his appeals and was denied parole. He faced the bleak reality that he would never be exonerated and perhaps never be released from prison.

I believe that Providence plays a major role in our lives. It did in Jeff's. He borrowed *Chicken Soup for the Prisoner's Soul* from the prison library and read a story I had written. Jeff checked my credentials at the back of the book and discovered my memoir. He contacted the publisher and told her his story. She contacted a mutual friend, Claudia, an advocate for the wrongly accused. She took up Jeff's cause and convinced the Innocence Project to handle his case, although they had previously turned down Jeff's request to work on his behalf.

The Innocence Project then persuaded the district attorney to run the existing DNA evidence from the original crime scene, which did not match Jeff's through the database. The result proved Jeff's innocence and revealed the actual guilty man was a prisoner serving life for another murder. Jeff, now thirty-three, was released from prison in 2006.

I get goose bumps every time I think about Jeff and how my writing played a role in setting him free. I want the rest of his life to be so special that he will forget the desolation of those sixteen years in prison. I believe that because of Jeff's own persistence, he will have a successful future. But I also want his story to motivate others to realize that horrible mistakes can be made even by well-meaning people. Today, Jeff is attending college. He is also advocating for changes in the criminal justice system so that others may not have to go through what he did.

Jeff taught me that we never know what small act of ours will make a difference. We can also learn three other lessons from Jeff's story. The first lesson is that the difference we make in someone's life doesn't have to be a grand gesture, because mine was not. All I did was write a story. The second is to never give up. Jeff persevered against the most severe odds that anyone could face, and he won. The third lesson is that there is no amount of money we can earn that can replace the reward we get from giving back a person's life.

I may never win the Pulitzer prize or be on anyone's bestseller list. But how many of those authors can say that something they wrote played a part in giving a man's life back to him?

[EDITOR'S NOTE: *For more information on the Innocence Project, contact 100 Fifth Avenue, 3rd Floor, New York, NY 10011; e-mail: info@innocenceproject.org; website: www.innocence project.org; phone: 212-364-5340.*]

❧ ❧

I wish I could do an hour of wall-time or clean the show-ers to get a month taken off my sentence, but that isn't realistic. Instead I must make the strongest effort within myself to be as responsible with my life as possible. I can't afford to cheat and cut corners anymore. That has only brought me pain.

                                        John Schmidt

Returning to Normalcy

STELLA SHEPARD

When he sentenced me to a six-year term, the judge declared, "I'm returning you to normalcy, Stella!"

Returning to prison, I felt no allegiance to the other prisoners and saw no purpose for the next six years of my life. *What person in here would ever believe that I actually tried to transition into mainstream society or that I had a burning desire to succeed . . . not to fail? Who would be here to listen to me and comfort me? Would anyone give me encouragement?*

Prison had lost its magic. I'd forgotten the mandatory counts, the sickening smell of disinfectant used to clean the cells, or the piercing voices of the officers bellowing out absurd commands from morning to night. I had forgotten how to be a "prisoner."

How can I accept this situation? How will I move from this paralyzing place of self-hate and loathing to the realization of why I'm here, to seek change and to eventually find peace? These questions plagued me for months, until one day, while on the yard, I encountered another inmate, Barbara. She reflected the young woman I'd once been. After we talked for a few minutes, she said, "My children would never be labeled 'suckers' or grovel for a job!"

Barbara was possessed with the warped desire to rule over this criminal underworld of deception and illusion, determined to continue stealing and hustling. As I watched and listened to her, the faces of my two young daughters appeared before my eyes. I wondered, *How are they developing without my guidance? Would they too resort to crime?* It was then that I became determined to make a difference in this young woman's life. Perhaps it was out of guilt for having left my daughters again or maybe it was the spirit of God moving in my life. In any case, it became my mission to transform both Barbara and myself.

From that day forward, I transformed myself into her big sister and then into her mother figure. I proudly watched as Barbara obtained her GED certificate. I applauded her efforts at succeeding in many prison programs geared toward changing her behavior. Like a mother eagle, I protected and guarded her, all the while realizing my own freedom. It was through mentoring her that I also realized my true purpose.

During this period of time I developed the ACT-UP program, which helps female prisoners develop character in order to regain their footing, which is crucial for reentry into society. Barbara was equally proud of me when the Ohio Department of Corrections approved my idea for a reentry program.

Barbara and I both gained a sense of purpose. We came to realize that it was only through unselfishly giving of ourselves that we could return to normal.

[EDITOR'S NOTE: *For more information on ACT-UP Character Building Program, e-mail: stellashepard@yahoo.com.*]

❧ ❧

I have always believed, and I still believe, that whatever good or bad fortune may come our way, we can always give it meaning and transform it into something of value.

Hermann Hesse

A Plan and a Purpose

STEPHEN GRUBER

As a jail chaplain, I explain to inmates that there is only one thing that separates them from me—three inches of steel and glass. I am privileged to meet inmates from all walks of life and diverse backgrounds. While I wear many hats and attempt to be all things to all people, I remain keenly aware that I'm not able to help everyone. In my role as a Christian chaplain, I strive to help inmates come to an understanding of the Scriptures. My continual prayer is that they come to know the Savior in a personal way.

When inmates want to speak to me, they fill out a request slip. One day, Larry sent me an urgent plea. "Please come quickly."

When I receive such a request, it's often because the inmate wants reading material, such as a Bible, Torah, or Koran, which I gladly provide. I never presume to know the reason why an inmate asks to see me; it could be because a parent is ill, a child has been hospitalized, or a spouse has died. The sooner I can get to that inmate to help may mean the difference between life and death. Inmates experiencing emotional loss can become suicidal.

Clutching Larry's request slip, I hurried to his housing unit, navigated through the security doors, and took a seat in the dayroom. Through the row of windows, I watched as Larry walked through the last security door. His face turned red. Making no effort to hide his emotion, he burst into tears as he entered the meeting room and sat down. Even though we were separated by steel and glass, Larry sat and wept for what seemed like a long time. After sitting quietly for a while, I asked, "Is this a good time to talk? I can come back."

"I have to talk to you *now,* Chaplain." From his expression, I instinctively knew what he was going to say. "The most incredible thing happened. God is more real to me now than ever. When I came to jail, I knew He still loved me, but the other day as I read the Psalms, I heard His voice telling me that He wants me here. It was as though God held up a mirror to me, and suddenly I saw all my sins. I couldn't take it. I broke down and cried. It was amazing."

Choking back tears, Larry continued. "The Lord said He wants me *here.* He wants to teach me some important lessons while I pay for my crimes. I only have six more months left on my sentence, but I feel at peace. I know God has a plan and a purpose for my life."

Larry and I talked a while longer. I referred him to other Scripture passages. Before Larry was transferred to another jail, we met frequently. He is due to be released soon. I will continue to work with him after his release, helping him get a job and become part of a local church community.

Much of Larry's success hinges on his determination to conquer his drug addiction, set realistic goals for his future, and the willingness of good people on the outside to reach out and help him. I will be one of those people.

It is one of the most beautiful compensations of this life that no man can sincerely try to help another without helping himself.

Emerson

Prison Volunteers—A Loving Example

CHRISTOPHER MOORE

For your unselfish love,
Shown in every way.
For the warmth of your smile,
And the things that you say.

For your listening ear,
And your giving heart.
Your compassionate hugs,
And your tears when we part.

For the strength of your prayers,
And the wisdom you share.
Your encouraging letters,
Showing us that you care.

Volunteers—how we love you.
And we want you to know,
By the seeds you have planted,
We continue to grow.

If you touch just one person in your lifetime and show you care, providing hope and meaning, you have lived a life of purpose worth living.

James Guy

A Divine Intervention

KURT R. MOSHER

To many people it may sound strange, but I really believe
God saved my life by sending me to prison. Prior to my
arrest, my drug use and lifestyle had worked me into a constant state of paranoia and an attitude bent on self-destruction.

When I was first incarcerated, I was still too blinded by the
drugs to understand this was a divine intervention, not just
another chapter in my tortured journey through addiction.
Prison turned out to be nothing short of a miracle.

As my mind and body detoxified, I started to look past the
violence and degradation. Underneath the misery were some
of the most compassionate acts of kindness I have ever
experienced. As my head cleared, I became deeply involved
with the Narcotics Anonymous group inside the Oregon State
Penitentiary. Becoming a part of the recovering community
and having the opportunity to serve was a genuine life-
changing experience.

Inside the walls of prison you live in a world of extremes—
on one hand you have intense violence and callous criminal-
ity, but on the other end of the spectrum, you have deep
sharing of understanding, strength, and hope.

I was blessed to be part of a group where, amid the chaos and
insanity, I heard some of the most heartfelt, insightful, and sincere
testimonies to the devastation that addiction inflicts on individuals and their families. I was grateful to be able to experience my
own recovery and to help others go through the healing process.

Soon after my release, a family friend who does construction and handyman services gave me a job. I was definitely a fish out of water with absolutely no experience in this field, but with a lot of patience on the part of many people around me and the grace of God, eventually I went out on my own and am now the proud owner of a landscaping and property maintenance company. I currently have one employee, in addition to myself. My goal is to hire people recovering from substance abuse and transitioning back into life.

I am also very involved in my community doing volunteer work for a group called No Meth, Not in My Neighborhood, sharing my story of tragedy and success with diverse groups in my area. This month I am scheduled to speak to a group of about eighty high school kids. I hope my testimony at least plants a seed, stimulates thought, or encourages those who may be struggling.

In addition, I am involved in my church. I have to admit that I have been truly blessed and never imagined a life so full and rewarding. God does work in mysterious ways.

I can't help but think that God put me in prison, not only to save the public from the monster drugs turned me into but also to exercise His own unique form of vocational training.

[EDITOR'S NOTE: *For more information on Narcotics Anonymous World Services, Inc., contact P.O. Box 9999, Van Nuys, CA 91409; phone: 818-773-9999; website: www.na.org.*]

We are free to change if we want to. Regardless of our criminal past and former behaviors, we can remake ourselves and claim a new life.

Matt Bader

Days of Laughter

TONI CARTER

Where would any of us be without laughter? It was laughter that got me through my workdays at Folsom State Prison for sixteen years. Laughter also got plenty of my students through their days. The average day was plagued with major and minor interruptions from alarms to verbal altercations. It took a great deal of teacher creativity and patience to motivate students in order to make the learning process work.

I declared my classroom a laughter zone, and students respected this mission. I did not explain this to staff, however. Judging from the stares observed in my classroom windows, it became obvious that others felt we were having too much fun! Onlookers would often stop to peer through the windows, probably wondering, *What could possibly be so much fun?*

Some of the comments I got later on confirmed my suspicions. "What did you do today, Ms. Carter?" "I kept hearing laughter and had to see what was going on." "If I let my students make that much noise, it probably means they're up to no good." "Whenever I'm missing a student, I know I'll find him in your room."

Following a personal brainstorm, I introduced the concept of "Flying As." During the later part of the seven-hour school day, I noticed the students tended to become drowsy, almost comatose. The two fifteen-minute breaks with no physical recreation to keep their blood circulating was a challenge. I announced to the class, "Whenever I'm delivering instruction at the board and you catch me making a mistake, whomever catches the mistake gets an automatic A." To my surprise, I suddenly had alert students who got As for the first time in their lives. They began paying close attention.

One day my students were working on a geography lesson. One young man who had recently been assigned to class seemed overly cautious and distrustful. I soon learned why— he had spent approximately eight years in "administrative segregation," a.k.a, "the hole." He was leery of everyone and did not like being in crowded places like classrooms. It took several weeks for him to settle into our daily routine.

One day, I observed him carefully studying the map. I took my eyes off of him for a moment, and when I turned back, he was standing in front of my desk upset with the error he found in the geography book. He wanted a "Flying A" for finding a big mistake. He said according to that map, Las Vegas was in Nev-i-dah. I said, "That's right—Las Vegas is in Nevada."

He wondered aloud, "How could that be? I thought Las Vegas was in California. Do you mean to tell me that when I went to Las Vegas, I was in a different state?" He was mystified! He had always believed he never left California.

He smiled over this revelation and decided that perhaps there was something to this education stuff. I laughed and he joined in—the ice of distrust had melted. His thirst for learning took off, and he became one of the best students in class, with his head always in a book.

Learning what motivated these men to want to learn kept me excited about teaching in prison, and became my *raison d'être* [reason for being].

About to Give Up

TOM LAGANA

Whenever I check into a hotel, I routinely ask, "Where's a good place to eat? What sights should I see while I'm here?" My next question, "Could you please give me directions to the local jail?" typically produces an interesting reaction or two. Right on cue, I produce a copy of *Chicken Soup for the Prisoner's Soul* and reveal, "I'm the coauthor."

The first few months I tried this, I was amazed to find the hotel staff had a particular interest in the title and subject matter—some were even eager to confide a personal account about a friend or relative who was serving time.

It takes advance planning to obtain permission and security clearance in order to present programs to inmates. I'm usually successful in gaining admittance to most correctional facilities so I can offer a measure of encouragement wherever I can.

Several years ago, my wife, Laura, and I celebrated our anniversary by vacationing in Maui. In addition to enjoying ourselves, we arranged to present a program to female inmates at the Maui Community Correctional Center. The total involvement and overwhelming energy of the thirty or so women in attendance was a spiritual experience for us all.

But not all of my visits behind bars are this positive. One exceptionally hot summer several years ago, I was beckoned to the Southern states several times to present corporate seminars and keynotes.

While planning one of these trips, I began looking for

correctional facilities that might welcome a visitor. After discovering that there was a prison within three miles of my hotel, my hopes dissolved when countless attempts to make contact with them proved futile.

At the same time, a prison chaplain in an adjacent North Carolina city asked me to present a keynote speech to a group of prison volunteers. When I told him about my unsuccessful attempts to gain admittance to the prison near my hotel, he offered to make arrangements for me. "If that's what you want to do, Tom," he replied, "then I'll make that happen. Don't worry. I'll arrange everything." Before long the date was set, and we agreed to meet at my hotel before the program.

After arriving at the Raleigh airport, I settled into my hotel room and enjoyed a refreshing night's sleep. The next evening, after conducting a full-day seminar, we drove to the prison. I was hopeful this event would be inspirational for the inmates, perhaps giving them an ounce of hope, a glimpse of the outside world, or a few blessed moments of relief from the dreary routine.

As we entered the facility, my feelings of hope turned into disappointment. No staff were there to greet us or help. In fact, I soon discovered, no more than a feeble attempt was made to inform the inmates of my program.

We were ushered into a cavernous cafeteria in disarray from dinner, as evidenced by the chaotic arrangement of tables and scattered remnants of food that served as "fly magnets."

I thought, "What am I doing here in a North Carolina prison, on one of the hottest days on record, being upstaged by gigantic, rattling fans?" On top of everything else, only twelve inmates showed up—six left soon after realizing free books weren't part of this program.

I thanked the chaplain for his kind efforts and said good night. Sitting in my car, I wondered, "Why did I even bother? I could be relaxing at the hotel. I've been speaking all day, my feet hurt, and tomorrow I'll be up early again." After the seminar, feeling disheartened and about to renounce all thoughts of ever visiting another prison, I boarded my plane in Raleigh. I couldn't wait to share my demoralizing experience with my wife, Laura.

The next morning, I began sorting through my mail. I stopped cold when a Raleigh postmark caught my eye—it was a letter from an inmate. At first I thought it had something to do with my recent visit. I opened the letter and began reading. An inmate named Adam told me how he ended up in prison and about some of the events leading up to his fate—something prisoners don't normally disclose.

Reading further, I learned Adam had been arrested while earning his master's degree. He had been accepted into a doctorate program and was working two jobs to pay for tuition, rent, and food. When one of his jobs evaporated because his employer went bankrupt, Adam admitted he had made a horrendous error in judgment.

"I sold Ecstasy for only four months . . . but I got busted. After being drug-free for twenty-nine years, I screwed up my life, and now I'm facing a sentence of up to twenty years," he explained. "When I went to prison, suicide was a very real option. Soon after I was locked up, my mom sent me a book— *Chicken Soup for the Prisoner's Soul*. I read it in one day. It was then that I realized that I could make it. Here are some of the stories that were especially helpful to me."

Adam proceeded to cite specific stories that were instrumental in altering his self-destructive mind-set. "I thought my life was over. I'd thrown away eleven years of college and probably a chance at a doctorate. By the time I got to the story, 'Not a Mistake,' I realized that, while I had made a huge mistake, I am not a mistake. As the story mentions, 'Good people are sometimes capable of doing bad things and allow stupidity to overcome rational thought.' I pray twice daily. I ask the

Lord to touch my district attorney and judge with compassion and forgiveness, in hopes they will pass it on—not just to me, but to all who come before them. Because of your book, I thank God for every glorious day, whether behind bars or not—because it could be worse."

When I finished reading Adam's letter, I handed it to Laura, who was reading the newspaper across the breakfast table. Choking back the tears, I asked, "Sweetheart, would you read this and tell me what you think?"

"Sure." When she finished, Laura removed her glasses, looked me square in the eyes, and asked, "How does this letter make you feel?"

"It makes me feel like I'm doing what I'm meant to do."

THE IN SIDE by Matt Matteo

Reprinted by permission of Matt Matteo.

Your Unique Purpose: Discover Why the World Needs You

TOM LAGANA AND LAURA LAGANA

8.1 Describe the endeavors or tasks you see yourself pursuing during your incarceration that will help reveal your unique purpose in life.

8.2 What endeavors do you see yourself pursuing after your release?

8.3 What are your interests?

8.4 What do you do well? What are your strengths?

8.5 What skills would you like to improve on and sharpen?

8.6 Write two to three paragraphs completing the following statement: "My purpose in life is . . ."

Programs and Resources

Continue to grow and prosper. Plant seeds for a better future today, and one day you will reap a rich harvest. What programs are you currently engaged in? What programs have you already participated in?

Make a list of all programs that are available to you. Ask the appropriate staff members at your facility for approval to take them. Then attend as many as you can. Some of these may include: Alternatives to Violence (AVP), Alcoholics Anonymous (AA), Narcotics Anonymous (NA), Kairos, Toastmasters, carpentry, creative writing, Life Connections, Prison Fellowship Ministries, and Gangs Anonymous, to name a few.

When becoming part of a program, ask yourself: *Why do I want to attend? What do I hope to gain? What can I contribute to the class or program?*

TOM LAGANA AND LAURA LAGANA

Securing Financial Aid
for the Nontraditional Student

TROY EVANS

After spending more than seven years in federal prison, I was determined my time behind bars would not be wasted time. Education would be my saving grace. Even though my aspirations coincided with the elimination of federal Pell Grants for the incarcerated, I set out to secure funding through scholarships, grants, and foundation assistance. After six months of completing applications, writing essays, begging, selling, and pleading, I landed my first scholarship. By the time I walked out of prison, I had two degrees, both obtained with a 4.0 GPA and recognition on the dean's and president's lists. Below are suggestions to help the nontraditional student secure financial aid.

Correspond with the school or university you have chosen. This is the first step and the quickest way to land a scholarship. Most institutions offer some type of scholarship program or package through an alumni association, foundation, or sponsorship. Some people may choose to research what financial aid is available at several schools, making that the determining factor in deciding which school they will attend.

Apply for federal and state aid. Although the incarcerated do not qualify for either one, many scholarships you apply for in the future will require that you exhaust these two possibilities first.

Contact the Department of Commerce where you reside and where the school is located. Obtain a listing of civic and service clubs in their region (e.g., Kiwanis, Rotary, Lions, etc.) and personally contact each one. They frequently sponsor scholarships that are often earmarked for hard-luck cases, such as the incarcerated.

Associations in your area can be accessed using Internet search engines. Contact the public affairs division and inquire about what is available for someone in your situation. In particular, target nonprofit, social work, and groups that focus on helping others.

Churches and religious organizations in your vicinity some-times have money designated for hard-luck cases. Some church leaders have discretion on how this money is to be distributed. In some cases, the incarcerated fall into this category.

Private scholarships are available, based on every imagin-able criterion (e.g., the degree you seek, gender, race, religious background). Several good books list available private scholar-ships and grants nationwide: Peterson's *Scholarships, Grants and Prizes* and Daniel J. Cassidy's *Scholarships, Grants and Loans* each offer scholarships, ranging from several hundred dol-lars to thousands of dollars. When submitting an application, apply for everything you even remotely qualify for. The associa-tion that funded practically my entire academic career started with a private scholarship I didn't qualify for. They were so impressed with what I was trying to do that they made an excep-tion and awarded me a scholarship for one class, which ulti-mately led to supporting most of my academic career while I served my time.

The Internet has databases for thousands of public and pri-vate scholarships. If you do not have Internet access, ask a family member or friend to help with your research.

Public and private foundations and trusts are abundant. To maintain their tax-exempt status, they are required to give away a certain amount of funds annually. A portion of this money is allocated for education. Securing this funding may take months or years, but pursuing this possibility early on in your academic career is prudent. It can provide a large chunk of assistance and allow you to go on to complete additional degrees. An excellent resource is *Foundation Grants to Individuals,* published by the Foundation Center.

The essay is the most important part of securing financial aid. Applying for most scholarships will require that you write an essay, describing why you deserve it. Your application will be judged solely on what you write. Emphasize how you plan to use education as a way of turning a negative situation into a positive one, as well as turning your life around, thereby improving the likelihood of future success. Let the committee know that a private scholarship, or whatever you are applying for, is your only available source of funding. Also inform them that state and federal aid is not possible and that you are facing the last avenue that can help you live your dream. Sell yourself as someone who wants to turn their life around. Make certain your essay is in the acceptable format, with perfect spelling, grammar, and punctuation.

A's are crucial, particularly in the first few courses. As you apply for scholarships later on, you will want to send your transcripts and report cards, along with your application and essay. This history of what you have done with scholarship money in the past shows the committee members that you are serious about education *and* that you are determined to turn your life around. You must be able to demonstrate that their money is being spent on a worthy investment.

This overview should help you get started. There are many reasons you should secure funding for your education while serving your time. It is simply a matter of *beating the bushes*. The money *is* out there, but to make it happen, the desire and effort *must* be first. If you are serious about obtaining an education via correspondence during your incarceration, I'm living proof it *can* happen. Good luck and go *shake those bushes*.

[EDITOR'S NOTE: *For more information, check www.fafsaon line.com/financial-aid-application and www.college-scholar ships.com. Reference:* Prisoners' Guerrilla Handbook to Correspondence Programs in the United States and Canada *by Jon Marc Taylor. Contact: Biddle Publishing Company, 13 Gurnet Road, PMB 103, Brunswick, ME 04011, www.biddle audenreed.com.*]

Selecting a College or University

BRANDON T. LAGANA

When selecting a college or university from which to earn a degree, be sure it is accredited regionally by one of the six regional accrediting bodies (listed below). Virtually all of the state universities and well-known private colleges are regionally accredited. National accreditation or accreditation by another agency other than the six listed could become problematic, if you wish to have credits transferred and to equate them to course requirements at another college. The bottom line is to pursue degrees through regionally accredited colleges whenever possible.

Courses from a college you previously attended will also be considered by the new college at which you wish to take courses. Previous coursework can sometimes count toward your total credits as general electives, while at other times they may count toward your major or general education courses.

An important form to complete in the financial aid process is called the Free Application for Federal Student Aid (FAFSA). The form can be completed online or in a limited paper version. Their official website is www.fafsa.ed.gov.

Financial aid typically is discussed among the general public as assistance when one's income is insufficient to cover the cost of college. Financial aid comes in three different forms:

1. Need-based aid is based on income (can be grants that do not have to be paid back or loans that must be repaid).

2. Scholarships and other forms of merit aid are based on one's involvement, leadership, and life experience. These do not have to be repaid.

3. Grants can be based on income needs and merit. These do not have to be repaid.

The six regional accrediting bodies are:

1. New England Association of Schools and Colleges (NEASC).

2. Middle States Association of Colleges and Schools (MSACS).

3. Southern Association of Colleges and Schools (SACS).

4. North Central Association of Colleges and Schools (NCACS).

5. Northwest Commission on Colleges and Universities (NWCCU).

6. Western Association of Schools and Colleges (WASC).

Education is a valuable key to opening the door of success. You have everything to gain by going for it. I wish you the best.

One's mind, once stretched by a new idea, never regains its original dimensions.

Oliver Wendell Holmes

Making a Personal Game Plan

JOSEPH CHIAPPETTA, JR.

Getting out of prison is a stressful experience no matter how prepared you may believe you are. In effect, you are moving from one type of culture to another. To lessen the shock and increase your odds of success, you should draft a personal checklist tailored to your specific needs. Many inmates put this process off or dismiss the notion of writing things down at all. When a person leaves prison, hundreds of distractions can derail any plan. Writing down your plans keeps you focused. It's like making a list to take to the grocery store. You stick to that list; otherwise you end up with a cart full of stuff you really don't need and forget to pick up the things you wanted in the first place. "Getting out" is just like that. If you don't create a list and work through that list, many things simply will not get done.

Your personal game plan is a list of realistic and attainable short-term goals. Everybody's long-term goals are roughly the same: not returning to prison, getting a job, taking care of or starting a family. It's the specific short-term goals we set for ourselves that pave the way to our long-term ones. One of the best ways to start is by creating lists that cover each day of your first two to four weeks after release. Write each list to cover three to four days at a time. Remember not to assume you have jobs or other resources waiting for you. Just because somebody promises you something, even if they are family, it's not a guarantee. Many ex-inmates reoffend after going home to broken promises. You must make a plan that relies on you and what you can do. There are many resources available out there. One-Stop Career Centers have lists of places to obtain employment, housing, food, clothes, tools, and transportation. Your "Game Plan Checklist" for the first four days should look something like this:

Day 1

- Call my family
- See my parole officer
- Check in at halfway house
- Set up transportation (public, friends, family)
- Pick up/purchase clothes and hygiene items

Day 2

- Get driver's license
- Get Social Security card
- Go to One-Stop Center to register for services, set up federal bonding, update my résumé, and set up job interviews
- Set up a free e-mail account

Day 3

- See my family
- Set up job interviews
- Open a checking account
- Get a copy of my credit report

Day 4

- Go to interviews
- See children
- Go to a 12-step or other support group meeting
- Make phone calls and e-mail my networking contacts

Notice that things like going to the old neighborhood, having a party with old friends, or looking for a date do not make the list. The hard truth is that if you do not get yourself squared away first before worrying about recreation, your odds of violating parole or reoffending goes through the roof. This is common sense and your choice. You may not get everything done on this timetable, but you can add and delete tasks as you go. The key is writing everything down and steadily getting things done. Before you know it, you are closer to those long-term goals.

Networking is developing a pool of people who can help you, provide you with useful information, or even introduce you to others willing to help. Making a list of names and contact information for everybody who gives you any positive feedback is the beginning of this networking. People you should add are your friends, family, clergy, and even prospective employers who liked you during the interview but couldn't hire you right away. It's all about who you are now and what you can do with your future, not just where you've been and how you got there.

Get involved in a prerelease or transitional-living program. This is the best thing you can do to maximize your chances of success. No other program gives you more tools and current vital information than a reentry program.

Get started. Start making your personal game plan now. Make as many arrangements as you can before you get out. Waiting until the last minute is a plan for failure.

Give yourself time to adjust. Don't try to get everything done on the first day. Be sure to take time alone with family and close friends. Be patient with yourself and understand that it might take you a while to reach your goals. You may feel depressed or overwhelmed. These feelings are normal. Just be patient with yourself, stay positive, and follow your plan.

Many transitional-living students are focused on small business ownership, credit repair, real estate ownership, and other financial matters. However, most of them learn that it's the simple things that matter most. The simple habit of writing things down and carrying out those tasks is the foundation to any future success.

[EDITOR'S NOTE: *For more information on One-Stop*

Career Centers, visit the CareerOneStop website: www.career onestop.org; e-mail: info@careeronestop.org; phone: 877- 348-0502.]

❧ ☙

To meet the challenges after my release, I set goals, stayed in touch with my children, worked on my relationship with my parents, worked hard, spent less than I earned, and avoided temptations to stray off course. I succeeded by limiting my priorities to the important things, solving problems as they come up, and focusing on my goals.

Matt Bader

About Tom Lagana

Tom Lagana believes that one person can make a difference. He is dedicated to living a positive, successful life and helping others to do the same.

When Tom was a child, his mother, a registered nurse, often volunteered with the American Red Cross and would take him along with her. Influenced and inspired by her loving example, Tom continued his own volunteering activities and, as a teenager, started with fund-raising projects for his school. In his adult years, he served to help solicit funding from corporations and employees for the United Way of Delaware.

He has served extensively in the prison system throughout the United States, working with inmates. He is a volunteer in the Emergency Department of Wilmington Hospital, part of the Christiana Care Health System in Delaware.

In 1994, he was honored as a recipient of the Jefferson Award for outstanding public service. He and his wife, Laura, have two grown sons and two grandsons.

Tom graduated from Villanova University in Pennsylvania with a degree in electrical engineering and worked as an engineer for more than thirty years. In his corporate career, he was often asked to deliver technical presentations. As his passion for inspiring others evolved, he learned the value of sharpening his public speaking skills.

Tom has facilitated more than 1,000 personal development and management presentations nationally and internationally. Through his refreshingly humorous presentations, laced with innovative audience interactions, Tom inspires people everywhere to become their best.

Tom's life experiences have led him to coauthor two highly successful books in the bestselling Chicken Soup for the Soul series, including *Chicken Soup for the Prisoner's Soul*. He and Laura are coauthors of *Chicken Soup for the Volunteer's Soul, Serving Time, Serving Others,* and *The Quick and Easy Guide to Project Management.*

Tom Lagana
P.O. Box 7816, Wilmington, DE 19803
302-475-4825
e-mail: Tom@TomLagana.com
website: www.TomLagana.com

About Laura Lagana

Laura Lagana is an author, professional speaker, nurse, and volunteer. She is a coauthor of *Chicken Soup for the Volunteer's Soul; Serving Time, Serving Others;* and *The Quick and Easy Guide to Project Management.* She is also author/editor of *Touched by Angels of Mercy* and a frequent Chicken Soup for the Soul contributing author.

At age sixteen, undecided about which career path to choose, she heeded a friend's advice and became a candy striper at a local hospital to observe the role of the professional nurse, advice that helped her decide. Five years later, Laura graduated from the Bryn Mawr Hospital School of Nursing in Bryn Mawr, Pennsylvania.

During her twenty-eight years as a registered nurse, Laura harvested scores of unforgettable experiences.

A volunteer for most of her life, she admits to reaping immeasurable rewards and gaining insight into the human condition. Today she is an intensive care unit volunteer with the Christiana Care Health System in Wilmington, Delaware.

In 1997, steered by the winds of change, Laura made a transition from a career in nursing to that of writing and speaking, where she savors the opportunity to follow her lifelong passion as she combines the best of all three worlds. Laura works with her husband, Tom (coauthor of *Chicken Soup for the Prisoner's Soul*), in their own business, which often takes them across the United States, presenting and facilitating seminars for clients on both sides of the razor wire.

Applying the knowledge gleaned from her lived-life experiences, Laura delights in helping people become their best.

Laura Lagana
P.O. Box 7816, Wilmington, DE 19803
302-475-4825
e-mail: Laura@LauraLagana.com
website: www.LauraLagana.com

Contributing Authors and Cartoonists

Sue Ellen Allen is an author, speaker, and activist. Being in prison with stage 3B breast cancer was a strange blessing—the defining moment of her life. Despite the odds, she survived. Now her motto is, "Been there, done that. How can I help?" Contact her at sueellen2008@hotmail.com or write her c/o Carolyn Cooper, Suite 11, Box 118, 2023 W. Guadulupe Road, Mesa, AZ 85202.

Jay Angelo teaches the "Real Men, Real Talk" class for fellow inmates in conjunction with the nonprofit organization H.O.P.E. (Helping Our Prisoners Elevate). Over the years, he has facilitated various study groups and looks forward to being a motivational speaker and counselor for at-risk youth, especially those who have incarcerated parents. He may be reached at James White #219184, Parr Highway Correctional Facility, 2727 East Beecher St., Adrian, MI 49221.

Leland J. Balber is a songwriter/singer, writer, publicist, and public speaker. He also is a child and adolescent development specialist. In addition to his career in the arts, he has worked as a psychotherapist, substance abuse rehabilitation counselor, and sales professional. He can be reached via e-mail at Lelandj@bellsouth.net.

Leonard Baylis was a charter member of Walking Tall Toastmasters at Gander Hill Prison in Wilmington, Delaware. He is a writer and illustrator, using his experience and ability to advocate for those who suffer learning and developmental disorders. He may be contacted via e-mail at LeonardBaylis@aol.com.

Ray Benich served a sixteen-year mandatory sentence at Gander Hill Prison in Wilmington, Delaware. He is a member of the American Society of Composers, Authors, and Publishers (ASCAP), and has recorded four LP record albums with United Artists. He may be reached via e-mail at ray@damnationofadamblessing.net; or website: www.damnationofadamblessing.net.

Roy A. Borges is a 1998 first place Amy Award winner and author of *Faith and Love Behind Prison Fences*. He is a contributing author in *Chicken Soup for the Prisoner's Soul*. He may be contacted at #029381, Mayo Correctional Institution, 8784 West US 27, Mayo, FL 32066.

Christopher Bowers is serving time in Western Missouri Correctional Center. He is coauthor of *Lost Innocence: Understanding Youth Who Kill*, which may be ordered through Lost Innocence, c/o Julio Padilla, P.O. Box 9155, Shawnee Mission, KS 66201; e-mail: saveouryouth@hotmail.com; website: www.YouthWhoKill.com.

Douglas Burgess is serving a life sentence for a crime he committed while on leave from the Marine Corps in 1984. He is committed to atoning for his past misdeeds through programs benefiting homeless shelters, food banks, and youthful offenders. He is currently writing his second book and is a contributing author in *Chicken Soup for the Prisoner's Soul* and *Serving Time, Serving Others*. Contact him at #178559 KCF, 16770 S. Watertower, Kincheloe, MI 49788.

Allison "Tammy" Butler is an inmate at a Pennsylvania state correctional facility. She is currently working on her memoir. Her story, "I Am Free," is an excerpt from her book. She may be contacted via e-mail at allisonbutl@msn.com or write her at #OL8397, 451 Fullerton Ave., Cambridge Springs, PA 16403.

Mary V. Leftridge Byrd, a criminal justice professional of more than thirty years, is a former warden of men's and women's prisons. She serves as deputy secretary with the Washington State Department of Corrections and held the same position with the Pennsylvania Department of Corrections. Her leadership philosophy is to "Do justly, love mercy, walk humbly." She is a contributing author in *Serving Time, Serving Others*. Contact her via e-mail at mvlbyrd@aol.com.

Charles Carkhuff is a published poet and cartoonist. Several of his cartoons are published in *Chicken Soup for the Prisoner's Soul*. He has taught self-help groups and continues to help others find their inner strength and reach their full potential. Contact him through e-mail at CharlesCarkhuff@mail.com.

Rod Carter is the director of the Restorative Justice Program at Queen's Theological College. He was formerly regional chaplain for the Correctional Service of Canada for five years. An ex-offender, he received a criminal pardon in 1977. He is a contributing author in *Chicken Soup for the Prisoner's Soul* and *Serving Time, Serving Others*. Contact him via e-mail at carterr@queensu.ca or write him at Queen's Theological College, 1000 University Ave., Kingston, Ontario K7L 3N6, Canada.

Toni Carter retired as a correctional teacher from Folsom State Prison. She is owner of GroovyMondays.biz, where she markets an elite line of nutritional products, working to increase awareness for living in good health. She is also a contributing author in *Chicken Soup for the Prisoner's Soul* and *Serving Time, Serving Others*. Contact her at P.O. Box 983, Roseville, CA 95678.

Michael Chernock is a management consultant during the week, but every other Sunday since 1995, he has teamed up with friends to conduct church services, baptisms, and share the Eucharist at the San Quentin hospital and HIV ward. He is also a contributing author in *Serving Time, Serving Others*. Contact him via e-mail at Michael@ChernockAssociates.com or visit his website: www.ChernockAssociates.com.

Joseph Chiappetta, Jr., is serving a thirty-five-year sentence in Arizona. He developed and facilitated a prerelease and employability course and has published a manual entitled *From Here to the Streets* (www.FromHereToTheStreets.com), a prerelease employability guide complete with lessons, materials, and forms, as well as the guide, "Report Card to Paychecks: Employability for Young Adults." He may be contacted via e-mail at joejr122@yahoo.com or write him at #161479, ASPC Eyman, Cook Unit, P.O. Box 3200, Florence, AZ 85232.

Grace Clark retired from teaching after fifty years. She was married to Robert, a United Methodist minister, until he passed away in late 2007. She has four children and eight grandchildren. Volunteering in prison ministry, Kairos, and Kairos Outside has brought her rewarding experiences. She can be contacted via e-mail at gobobclark@bellsouth.net.

Melissa L. Craft is a licensed independent social worker and has worked in the field of children and family mental health issues for more than twelve years as a therapist. She enjoys studying God's word through Bible study and helping others through life's difficult times, especially those involving their children. She may be contacted via e-mail at mlc75@scdmh.org.

Lynn Durham, RN, is a well-being coach who incorporates her experience as a professor of nursing education, author, columnist, professional speaker, and mother of three sons to help clients and audiences (live and on air) feel better. One corporate consultant dubbed her "a creative antidote to the everyday stressors of business . . . and life." She is a contributing author in *Touched by Angels of Mercy*. See her website: www.LynnDurham.com.

Troy Evans is a professional speaker, author, and ex-inmate. He is author of *From Desperation to Dedication: An Ex-Con's Lessons on Turning Failure into Success*. He is a contributing author in *Serving Time, Serving Others*. He may be contacted at The Evans Group, 3104 E. Camelback Road #436, Phoenix, AZ 85016; e-mail: troy@troyevans.com; website: www.troyevans.com.

Gary K. Farlow is a native Tar Heel with a juris doctor from Heed University. His works are in three Chicken Soup for the Soul books, *Serving Time, Serving Others,* and two poetic anthologies. He is author of *Prison-ese: A Survivor's Guide to Speaking Slang* and his poetry books, *Conferring with the Moon* and *After Midnight*. He may be contacted at #0125977, Nash Correctional Institution, P.O. Box 600, Nashville, NC 27856.

David J. Feddes is director of the Center for Advanced Studies, the academic and research arm of Crossroad Bible Institute (CBI; www.crossroadbible.org). CBI provides Christian distance education and discipleship to more than 40,000 students (primarily prisoners) in sixty countries. Before coming to Crossroad Bible Institute, David hosted the international *Back to God Hour* radio program for sixteen years.

Charles T. Fehil once led a notorious white supremacy gang in the Illinois prison system. After turning his life over to the Lord, he now helps others find hope and inspiration. Contact him at B-10407, Greene County Work Camp, P.O. Box C, Roodhouse, IL 62802 or e-mail him at CharlesFehil@mail.com.

Brian M. Fisher once served time in Iowa. While incarcerated, he graduated from the InnerChange Freedom Initiative program. He has also taken part in several writing classes. He is forever grateful for his family's loving support. He may be contacted via e-mail at mrbrian321@yahoo.com.

Ken Fox loves his family and is engaged to be married. He enjoys watching and playing football. His hobbies include reading and writing poetry, as well as crocheting. He loves to talk about the Bible. He may be contacted at #233713, West Shoreline Correctional Facility, 2500 S. Sheridan Dr., Muskegon Heights, MI 49444.

Shawn Fox is serving life without parole and has dedicated the rest of his life to helping others. He is a self-taught artist, and his website (www.shawnfox.us) displays some of his work. He may be contacted through e-mail at fox6175@comcast.net or at #6175068, Oregon State Penitentiary, 2605 State St., Salem, OR 97310.

William G. L. Francis, Jr., was born in Harlem, New York, in 1971 into a Caribbean American family. He is a high school graduate, and while incarcerated, he completed courses in business, law, and private investigation. He has helped hundreds of fellow prisoners earn their GEDs and high school diplomas. Contact him via e-mail at finesse2201@hotmail.com.

SuEllen Fried is the cofounder of a program that sponsors groups in all eleven Kansas correctional facilities. She has been a volunteer with the Kansas Department of Corrections for thirty-five years. She is the coauthor of two books: *Bullies & Victims* and *Bullies, Targets & Witnesses*. Contact her at the website: www.bullysafeusa.com; via e-mail at suellenfried@hotmail.com; or at P.O. 8527, Shawnee Mission, KS 66208.

Steven D. Gaub is a husband, father, and grandfather. He holds several college degrees and is a retired army veterinary corps officer in private practice. He has been an active churchman all of his years and has served on Kairos weekends for the last seventeen years. He may be contacted via e-mail at stevengaub@aol.com.

Dale Gaudet has been a Toastmaster for many years and was one of the first inmates to ever receive the Distinguished Toastmasters award. He enjoys the outdoors and is active in Catholic prison ministry as a peer minister. He has two stories published in *Chicken Soup for the Prisoner's Soul*. Contact him at #325242, State Police Barracks, 1400 West Irene Road, Zachary, LA 70791.

Randy Geer is a twenty-five-year veteran who currently works as a corrections administrator. He is the son of Lieutenant Bob Geer, who was killed in the line of duty at the Oregon State Penitentiary in April 1972. He may be contacted at Oregon Department of Corrections—Central Office, 2575 Center St. NE, Salem, OR 97301.

Jerry Gillies is a former journalist (NBC-New York) and author of six books on personal development, including the bestselling *Moneylove* and the upcoming *The Great Escape*. For more than twenty years, he conducted seminars and lectures across the United States, Canada, England, and South Africa. His stories are also in *Chicken Soup for the Prisoner's Soul* and *Serving Time, Serving Others*. Recently paroled from Folsom State Prison, he can be contacted via e-mail at JerryGillies@gmail.com or website: www.jerrygillies.net.

Stephen Gruber, Ph.D., is the author of *Hiding Jesus Through the Ages*. He teaches philosophy and religion at various universities. He also serves as a law enforcement chaplain and holds master's degrees in theology and history. He has a Ph.D. in philosophy and history. He may be contacted via e-mail at docgruber@yahoo.com.

James Guy was stricken with colon cancer two years after writing his story. He is now reunited with his wife and family. He is retired and working on a book, exploring the religious views of capital punishment. He may be contacted via e-mail at mlgjhg@verizon.com or write him at P.O. Box 271, Sharon, PA 16146.

Belinda Pitts Harrison is involved in many oil field organizations and activities. She loves children and recently became a certified foster mother. She loves to travel and stay busy. She has four children and seven grandchildren. She may be reached via e-mail at belindaharrison@c-gate.net or P.O. Box 2396, Laurel, MS 39442.

Kenneth E. Hartman is a nationally recognized, award-winning author who has worked for more than seventeen years to affect transformational change inside prison. He is currently working on a book about the process of *Doing Time*. He may be contacted at C-19449, CSP-LAC/A2-217L, P.O. Box 4430, Lancaster, CA 93539-4430 or visit his website: www.kennethehartman.com.

Nolan P. Holliday has served time in California prisons since the early 1970s for a total of twenty years. He enjoys drawing as well as writing poetry, songs, and stories. He hopes to become a successful writer. His interests include wildlife, sports, and travel. After his release, he will reside in Los Angeles County and may be contacted via e-mail at NolanHolliday@mail.com.

Jimmy Huff has a letter ministry and ministers in person to people in jails, prisons, and nursing homes. He may be contacted at Jimmy Huff Ministry, 130 West 6th St., Colorado City, TX 79512.

Brandon T. Lagana, Ed.D., was a prison volunteer during his undergraduate work in college. One story about his experience appears in *Chicken Soup for the College Soul* and *Chicken Soup for the Prisoner's Soul*. Dr. Lagana is director of admission at the University of Maine, Farmington. See website: www.farmington.edu.

Tova Langley is a twenty-two-year-old mother who served three years in prison. She greatly appreciates all the support she received from family, friends, and those who helped make it possible for her to turn her life around. She is now working toward her degree to become a medical assistant. She may be reached at Tova327@yahoo.com.

Dave LeFave has written numerous poems and prides himself on staying positive and trying to make the most of any situation. His poem "Wasted Time" is one of the most popular works in *Chicken Soup for the Prisoner's Soul*. Dave is also published in *Serving Time, Serving Others*. Contact him at #86651, CTCF, P.O. Box 1010, Canon City, CO 81215.

Jaye Lewis is an award-winning inspirational writer who lives and writes in the Appalachian Mountains. She is a Christian who often writes for Chicken Soup for the Soul books. You are invited to visit her website at www.entertainingangels.org for more of her inspirational stories.

Patricia H. Martin retired from the business world in 1998, and since then she has used her master's degree in professional writing in other ways, such as teaching adult education and in development for a nonprofit organization. She is grateful to spend time with her husband and their grown children. Her hobbies include bicycling and walking her dog. She may be contacted at martineq@verizon.net.

Matt Matteo is a writer, painter, cartoonist, and prisoner from Derry, Pennsylvania. He continues to improve his work and himself by contributing to many publications, including *Chicken Soup for the Prisoner's Soul*; *Chicken Soup for the Volunteer's Soul*; *Serving Time, Serving Others;* and *Touched by Angels of Mercy*. He welcomes mail at #BS-7345, 801 Butler Pike, Mercer, PA 16137.

Lois McGinnis is the mother of a large family. She has worked in advertising and public relations. In addition to serving as a hospital lay chaplain, for several decades she has led retreats and days of quiet reflection. She is the author of *The Way to Your True Self* and may be contacted via e-mail at elmac3@verizon.net.

Gregory A. McWilliams is coauthor of the upcoming book, *Po' Boy's Kitchen: What Has God Got Cooking Behind Prison Walls?* He may be contacted at #218520, Brunswick Correctional Center, 1147 Planters Road, Lawrenceville, VA 23868.

Patrick Middleton, Ph.D., is the first prisoner in the United States to earn his B.A., M.Ed., and Ph.D. in a classroom setting. His critically acclaimed book, *Healing Our Imprisoned Minds*, is being used in prison treatment programs in several states. He is the author of his childhood memoir, *Incorrigible*. Contact him at AK-3703, P.O. Box 244, Graterford, PA 19426.

Tekla Dennison Miller is a former warden of a men's maximum and a women's multilevel prison in Michigan. She is the author of two memoirs: *The Warden Wore Pink* and *A Bowl of Cherries*. She is also the author of *Life Sentences* and *Inevitable Sentences*. She is also a contributing author in *Chicken Soup for the Prisoner's Soul*. She is a national speaker on criminal justice reform and women's issues. See her website: www.TeklaMiller.com.

Dan Millstein is the founder of Visions for Prisons and the Peace in Prison project. Currently, Dan is gathering 108 Million Teachers of Peace for a One Day of Peace International Forgiveness Festival, December 21, 2012. He is author of *The One Minute Miracle*. He is a contributing author in *Chicken Soup for the Prisoner's Soul* and *Serving Time, Serving Others*. Contact him at P.O. Box 1631, Costa Mesa, CA 92628; e-mail: Dan@teacherofpeace.org; websites: www.teacherof peace.org and www.visionsforprisons.org.

Ken "Duke" Monse'Broten, pen name Edward Allen Lee, died on April 7, 2007. He is author of *Messages from the Heart,* coauthor *of Cissy's Magic*, and contributing author with five stories in *Chicken Soup for the Prisoner's Soul*. He also has stories in *Touched by Angels of Mercy* and *Serving Time, Serving Others*. Contact his former business manager via at nancysancarlos@comcast.net.

Christopher Moore is employed at the VA Medical Center in Lebanon, Pennsylvania, and is a member of Word of Faith Church. He was born in Philadelphia, Pennsylvania, and is the author of *A Few Words of Encouragement*, a book for Christians in recovery. He can be reached via e-mail at cmac5908@yahoo.com.

Kurt R. Mosher is divorced and the father of one daughter. He has a background in chemical dependency and domestic violence counseling. He is a recovering addict and ex-felon. He may be contacted at P.O. Box 4149, Salem, OR 97302.

Derrick K. Osorio was an evangelist and Christian writer. He was also the founder of the "Round Robin Platform Prayer." He died in June 2008.

Scott Paul-Bonham is a Presbyterian pastor who rejoices daily for his wife and teenage daughter and son. Since 1999, he has been a chaplain at the U.S. penitentiary in Terre Haute, Indiana. Currently he is program manager of the residential, faith-based Life Connections program.

Bob Pauley is a songwriter, author, screenwriter, speaker, and educator in the field of computer science. His writings examine truth and justice (and sometimes the lack of both) in the criminal justice system. He has written extensively on death row issues and may be contacted via e-mail at robertapauley@aol.com.

Roland Peck has been serving the men at San Quentin Prison since 1991. Kairos changed his life, and he dedicated his life to Christ. In 1992, he started the AIDS and HIV ministry, now serving all the men in the hospital. Contact him at P.O. Box

51, Clayton, CA 94517, or via e-mail at acepeck@aol.com.

Mark T. Pieczynski is a self-taught artist. He is a graphic designer working in the printing plant at Nash Correctional Institution. He may be contacted there at #0740861, P.O. Box 600, Nashville, NC 27856. Note that the North Carolina Division of Prisons has a policy prohibiting inmate-to-inmate correspondence.

Kyle "Quilly" Quilausing is a unique, caring, respectful, and considerate man. He is a Polynesian/Asian who was born in Hilo on the Big Island of Hawaii. He is currently incarcerated and making the best of his temporary confinement. He was raised in a loving household and owes his utmost gratitude to his beautiful mother. He can be contacted via e-mail at ichai@hawaiiantel.net or write him at Halawa Correctional Facility, 99-902 Moanalua Hwy., Aiea, HI 96701.

Bill Riggs, Ed.D., is an instructor at Abilene Christian University. He and his wife currently teach "Marriage and Parenting" and "Anger Management for Substance Abuse and Mental Health Clients" courses at a local prison. Contact Dr. Riggs by phone: 325-668-2007; website: www.prisonministry.net/frf; e-mail: fandfministries@yahoo.com; or at Free and Forgiven Ministries, Inc., P.O. Box 5442, Abilene, TX 79608.

Rose M. Robacker was a Franciscan nun and high school principal. Afterward, she taught college and married a Broadway singer, who died five years later from the effects of being a prisoner of war in North Korea. She is a prison volunteer for the Wayne Pike Adult Literacy Program and may be contacted through their office at 1406 N. Main St., Honesdale, PA 18431, or e-mail her at rosieem@pdt.net.

George T. Scanlon has been released after serving time at the Hillsboro County Jail, where he passed the time writing short stories about his personal experiences spanning fifty-three years. He may be contacted at P.O. Box 202, Pevely, MO 63070.

Courtney Christine Schuloff is now twenty-one years old. She was sentenced to "natural life" but is steadily working on her case. While in jail, she received her GED at age seventeen and spoke to juveniles like herself who were experiencing trouble with the law. She is becoming a law clerk and may be contacted at #154495, Lowell Correctional Institute, 11120 NW Gainesville Rd., Ocala, FL 34482-1479.

Stella Shepard is enrolled at Cleveland State University earning her bachelor's degree in sociology. She is executive director of ACT-UP, a character-building reentry program that has a less than 0.0098 percent recidivism rate and is approved by the Ohio Department of Corrections. ACT-UP is funded by a grant from the Cleveland Foundation. She may be contacted via e-mail at stellashepard@att.net.

Lily Sherman, an avid admirer of her parents, who are active volunteers, also enjoys volunteering. She and her husband, daughter, and special-needs son live in a small town in Washington State, where she works at their church as an administrative assistant. She may be contacted via e-mail at lily.sherman@gmail.com.

Jan Singleton has two sons and loves the Lord. Her hobbies include reading, volunteering, and music. She is a member of Oregon CURE (Citizens United for Rehabilitation of Errants) and may be contacted at P.O. Box 1021, Cornelius, OR 97113 or via e-mail: jansil@verizon.net.

Christian Snyder served time in New York and launched a career in freelance cartooning while incarcerated. He has been published in numerous magazines and trade journals. He is published in several Chicken Soup for the Soul books and *Serving Time, Serving Others*. Cartooning was a positive rehabilitative tool, and he is pursuing a full-time cartooning career now that he is released. Contact him at P.O. Box 58, Greenville, PA 16125.

Laurie E. Stolen is a certified jail manager and the director of contracts and inmate services at the Larimer County Detention Center, where she has worked since 1998. She is a wife and mother. She has a B.S. degree from Colorado State University and an M.A. degree from University of Northern Colorado. Contact her via e-mail at stolenle@larimer.org or write her at 2405 Midpoint Drive, Fort Collins, CO 80525.

Maleah Stringer is president of the Indiana chapter of the 2nd Chance at Life Greyhound Prison Program. Her column in the *Anderson (IN) Herald Bulletin* newspaper raises awareness concerning animal care and cruelty. She helped get state legislation regarding animal cruelty sponsored and passed by testifying before the Senate and House committee hearings. Contact her via e-mail at Maleahstringer@aol.com; or visit the website: www.inapl.org.

Karl B. Strunk has been serving life without parole since he was a youth of sixteen. He embraces writing as the most effective means of communication and expression. He enjoys gardening and volunteers his summers growing produce for community shelters. Contact him via e-mail at kabrst@yahoo.com; website: www.sixteenandlife.com.

Ann Edenfield Sweet is executive director and founder of Wings Ministry, a program for family members of inmates, and Wings for L.I.F.E.—Life-skills for Inmate Families & Education. She is author of *Family Arrested: How to Survive the Incarceration of a Loved One*. Contact her at AnnEdenfield@Wings Ministry.org; www.WingsMinistry.org; or 2270 B Wyoming NE #130, Albuquerque, NM 87112.

Carla Wilson, LMSW, has been a correctional deputy for more than sixteen years. She is an inspirational speaker and guided meditation facilitator in jails, prisons, churches, and educational institutions. She offers phone counseling for professionals and anyone adjusting to a loved one's addiction or incarceration. She is working on her first book, *What If I'm Right?* She may be contacted via e-mail at cwilson@connectionprinciple.com or at the website: www.connectionprinciple.com.

Dick Witherow came to know the Lord at age thirty-three after learning his wife had cancer. He served as chaplain of Gospel Rescue Mission in West Palm Beach, Florida, and later became its executive director. In 1990, he started Matthew 25 Ministries, a prison ministry whose main focus is aftercare. Contact him via e-mail at dick@matthew25ministries.org or website: www.matthew25ministries.org.

Robert A. Woodring is a proud father of three, a writer, an ex-auditor, and lover of all outdoor sports. He can be reached at #A449-736, Madison Correctional Institution, P.O. Box 740, London, OH 43140-0740.

Permissions

Note: The first copyright year is when the contributing author originally wrote the piece. Most material was edited for this book in 2007 and 2008. Material written by authors Laura Lagana and Tom Lagana are not included in this listing.

Front Matter

Foreword. Reprinted by permission of Mary V. Leftridge Byrd. © 2007, 2008 Mary V. Leftridge Byrd.

The Inmate's Affirmation. Reprinted by permission of Jerry Gillies. © 2004, 2008 Jerry Gillies.

Chapter 1

First Impressions. Reprinted by permission of Gary K. Farlow. © 2007, 2008 Gary K. Farlow.

Imagine. Reprinted by permission of Dave LeFave. © 2004, 2008 Dave LeFave.

Inside My World. Reprinted by permission of Courtney Christine Schulhoff. © 2004, 2008 Courtney Christine Schulhoff.

One in Thirty-Three. Reprinted by permission of Bob Pauley. © 2001, 2004, 2008 Bob Pauley.

Tough Questions, Honest Answers. Reprinted by permission of SuEllen Fried. © 2003, 2008 SuEllen Fried.

Tasting True Freedom. Reprinted by permission of Troy Evans. © 1987, 2008 Troy Evans.

The Vigilant CO. Reprinted by permission of George T. Scanlon. © 2007, 2008 George T. Scanlon.

My Perpetual Protector. Reprinted by permission of William G. L. Francis, Jr. © 2007, 2008 William G. L. Francis, Jr.

Chapter 2

Dime-store Paper. Reprinted by permission of Jay Angelo. © 2007, 2008 Jay Angelo.

"Mom and Dad." Reprinted by permission of Dave LeFave. © 2004, 2008 Dave LeFave.

Just Be a Parent. Reprinted by permission of Grace Clark. © 2007, 2008 Grace Clark.

The Best a Mom Can Do. Reprinted by permission of Belinda Pitts Harrison. © 2004, 2008 Belinda Pitts Harrison.

The Shape of an Angel. Reprinted by permission of Jan Singleton. © 2007, 2008 Jan Singleton.

You'll Never Cry Again. Reprinted by permission of Ray Benich. © 1998, 2008 Ray Benich.

Sunlight of My Soul. Reprinted by permission of Leland J. Balber. © 2006, 2008 Leland J. Balber.

What Do You Tell a Crying Mother? Excerpted and adapted with permission of Ken "Duke" Monse'Broten from *Messages From the Heart* by Edwin Allen Lee. © 1997, 2008 Kenneth Monse'Broten (pen name Edwin Allen Lee). © 1997 by Kenneth Monse'Broten, published by 1st Books in cooperation with Wino Publishing, pp. 40–43.

What Do You Say? Reprinted by permission of Tova Langley. © 2008 Tova Langley.

Why, Daddy? Reprinted by permission of Robert A. Woodring. © 2005, 2008 Robert A. Woodring.

The Power of Music. Reprinted by permission of Ann Edenfield Sweet. © 2007, 2008 Ann Edenfield Sweet.

A Man of Integrity. Reprinted by permission of Roy A. Borges. © 2007, 2008 Roy A. Borges.

Chapter 3
The Real Heroes. Reprinted by permission of Dale Gaudet. © 2006, 2008 Dale Gaudet.

What a Father Feels. Reprinted by permission of Jay Angelo. © 2006, 2008 Jay Angelo.

"The Echo of Tears." Reprinted by permission of Kurt R. Mosher. © 2005, 2008 Kurt R. Mosher.

Becoming Brutally Honest. Reprinted by permission of Douglas Burgess. © 2006, 2008 Douglas Burgess.

Afraid to Forgive. Reprinted by permission of Karl B. Strunk. © 2006, 2008 Karl B. Strunk.

Beyond Your Outdate. Reprinted by permission of Carla Wilson. © 2007, 2008 Carla Wilson.

The Prison Yogi. Reprinted by permission of Dan Millstein. © 2000, 2008 Dan Millstein.

Chapter 4
Nurse Bonnie. Reprinted by permission of Ken "Duke" Monse'Broten. © 1998, 2008 Ken "Duke" Monse'Broten. Excerpted and adapted with permission of Ken

"Duke" Monse'Broten from *Messages From the Heart* by Edwin Allen Lee. © 1997, 2008 Kenneth Monse'Broten (pen name Edwin Allen Lee). © 1997 by Kenneth Monse'Broten, published by 1st Books in cooperation with Wino Publishing, pp. 151–156.

Christmas Angel. Reprinted by permission of Charles Carkhuff. © 2000, 2008 Charles Carkhuff.

Entertaining Angels. Reprinted by permission of Jaye Lewis. © 2000 Jaye Lewis.

Blinded by the Light. Reprinted by permission of James Guy. © 2003, 2008 James Guy.

From Prison to Doctorate. Reprinted by permission of Bill Riggs. © 2006, 2008 Bill Riggs.

Silent Friends. Reprinted by permission of George T. Scanlon. © 2007, 2008 George T. Scanlon.

Lessons in Humanity. Reprinted by permission of Randy Geer. © 2007, 2008 Randy Geer.

Let's Party. Reprinted by permission of Tekla Dennison Miller. © 1996, 2007, 2008 Tekla Dennison Miller. Excerpted and adapted with permission of Tekla Dennison Miller from pages 185 and 187 of *The Warden Wore Pink* by Tekla Dennison Miller. © 1996 by Tekla Dennison Miller.

A Steel and Concrete Christmas. Reprinted by permission of Rod Carter. © 2007, 2008 Rod Carter.

My First Christmas in Prison. Reprinted by permission of Lily Sherman. © 2006, 2008 Lily Sherman.

Choosing Your Thoughts. Reprinted by permission of Lynn Durham. © 2007, 2008 Lynn Durham.

Practice What You Preach. Reprinted by permission of Douglas Burgess. © 2007, 2008 Douglas Burgess.

My Former Self. Reprinted by permission of Troy Evans. © 2000, 2007, 2008 Troy Evans.

Beyond the Walls. Reprinted by permission of Patricia H. Martin. © 1999, 2008 Patricia H. Martin.

Chapter 5
Little Did I Know. Reprinted by permission of Ken Fox. © 2007, 2008 Ken Fox.

Seeking Peace. Reprinted by permission of Kenneth E. Hartman. © 2007, 2008 Kenneth E. Hartman.

Journey of Faith. Reprinted by permission of Melissa L. Craft. © 2007, 2008 Melissa L. Craft.

Crisis of Faith. Reprinted by permission of Roland Peck. © 2007, 2008 Roland Peck.

"God's Loving Hands." Reprinted by permission of Kyle "Quilly" Quilausing. © 2007, 2008 Kyle "Quilly" Quilausing.

A Place Closer to God. Reprinted by permission of Grace Clark. © 2007, 2008 Grace Clark.

Love Conquers All. Reprinted by permission of Dick Witherow. © 2007, 2008 Dick Witherow.

Yuletide Santa. Reprinted by permission of Karl B. Strunk. © 2007, 2008 Karl B. Strunk.

The Artist. Reprinted by permission of Carla Wilson. © 2007, 2008 Carla Wilson.

The Lady and the Bird. Reprinted by permission of Derrick K. Osorio. © 2007, 2008 Derrick K. Osorio.

I Finally Saw the Light. Reprinted by permission of Jimmy Huff. © 2005, 2008 Jimmy Huff.

Chapter 6
"The Person You Once Knew." Reprinted by permission of Brian M. Fisher. © 2002, 2008 Brian M. Fisher.

Worthy of a Better Life. Reprinted by permission of Laurie E. Stolen. © 2007, 2008 Laurie E. Stolen.

Parting Sorrow. Reprinted by permission of Shawn Fox. © 2006, 2008 Shawn Fox.

Greyhounds in Prison. Reprinted by permission of Maleah Stringer. © 2006, 2007, 2008 Maleah Stringer.

"The Road to Nowhere." Reprinted by permission of Dave LeFave. © 2004, 2008 Dave LeFave.

Con Artists. Reprinted by permission of Leonard Baylis. © 2007, 2008 Leonard Baylis.

"Changed." Reprinted by permission of Nolan P. Holliday. © 2007, 2008 Nolan P. Holliday.

Free as a Bird. Reprinted by permission of Charles T. Fehil. © 2007, 2008 Charles T. Fehil.

Chapter 7
I'm Free. Reprinted by permission of Allison "Tammy" Butler. © 2007, 2008 Allison "Tammy" Butler.

Reading 101. Reprinted by permission of Rose M. Robacker. © 2006, 2008 Rose M. Robacker.

A Puddle and a Prayer. Reprinted by permission of Michael Chernock. © 1999, 2008 Michael Chernock.

Learning to Trust. Reprinted by permission of David J. Feddes. © 2007, 2008 David J. Feddes.

It Starts with Trust. Reprinted by permission of Patrick Middleton. © 2007, 2008 Patrick Middleton.

It's Never Too Late. Reprinted by permission of Sue Ellen Allen. © 2004, 2008 Sue Ellen Allen.

Just a Tear. Reprinted by permission of Steven D. Gaub. © 2007, 2008 Steven D. Gaub.

A Unique Request. Reprinted by permission of Scott Paul-Bonham. © 2007, 2008 Scott Paul-Bonham.

"Stones." Reprinted by permission of Leonard Baylis. © 2007, 2008 Leonard Baylis.

Chapter 8
Giving a Life Back. Reprinted by permission of Tekla Dennison Miller. © 2006, 2007, 2008 Tekla Dennison Miller.

Returning to Normalcy. Reprinted by permission of Stella Shepard. © 2001, 2008 Stella Shepard.

A Plan and a Purpose. Reprinted by permission of Stephen Gruber. © 2007, 2008 Stephen Gruber.

"Prison Volunteers—A Loving Example." Reprinted by permission of Christopher Moore. © 2007, 2008 Christopher Moore.

A Divine Intervention. Reprinted by permission of Kurt R. Mosher. © 2005, 2008 Kurt R. Mosher.

Days of Laughter. Reprinted by permission of Toni Carter. © 2007, 2008 Toni Carter.

Programs and Resources
Securing Financial Aid for the Nontraditional Student. Reprinted by permission of Troy Evans. © 2000, 2007, 2008 Troy Evans.

Selecting a College or University. Reprinted by permission of Brandon T. Lagana. © 2007, 2008 Brandon T. Lagana.

Making a Personal Game Plan. Reprinted by permission of Joseph Chiappetta, Jr. © 2007, 2008 Joseph Chiappetta, Jr. Excerpted from an article published in *Prison Living* magazine, pp. 10–11, volume 2, issue 3, 2007.

How to Obtain Funding for Our Books

Groups seeking free books may consider some of the following ways other facilities and agencies have obtained local funding:

1. Canteen fund; commissary fund
2. Inmate improvement fund; inmate benefit fund; inmate educational fund
3. Religious groups (e.g., church, diocese, etc.)
4. Service groups
5. Prison ministries
6. Corporations, individuals, and volunteers
7. Bookstores and discount stores (some have a community service fund)
8. Ask for funding
9. Ask again in a different way, and try a different person or group
10. Keep asking

Attention chaplains, librarians, counselors,
teachers, and other correctional staff:
For quantity discounts, matching grants, and
special offers, send an e-mail to
Tom@TomLagana.com or phone 302-475-4825.